BLACK & WHITE IN A RAINBOW WORLD

A Study in Jude

REALFAITH.COM

By Mark Driscoll

Black & White in a Rainbow World: A Study in Jude
© 2023 by Mark Driscoll

ISBN: 979-8-9884124-2-7 (Paperback)
ISBN: 979-8-9884124-3-4 (E-book)

Scripture quotations are from the ESV® Bible (The Holy Bible, English Standard Version®), copyright © 2001 by Crossway, a publishing ministry of Good News Publishers. Used by permission. All rights reserved. The ESV text may not be quoted in any publication made available to the public by a Creative Commons license. The ESV may not be translated in whole or in part into any other language.

All emphases in Scripture quotations have been added by the author.

No part of this publication may be reproduced, stored in a retrieval system, or transmitted in any form by any means, electronic, mechanical, photocopy, recording, or otherwise, without the prior permission of the publisher, except as provided for by USA copyright law.

CONTENTS

Real Groups 1

CHAPTER 1
Black & White in a Rainbow World 3

CHAPTER 2
10 Fun Facts from Jude 11

CHAPTER 3
11 Warnings Before Studying Jude. 19

CHAPTER 4
Jude Personal and Group Study Guide. 25

1. Are you a Real Christian?
(Jude 1-2). 27

2. Are you a Fake Christian?
(Jude 3-4). 34

3. Are you a Woke Christian?
(Jude 5-10). 40

4. What Does God Think of Progressive Christianity?
(Jude 11-16). .47

5. How to Stand Firm in a Woke World
(Jude 17-25). .54

Endnotes. 64
About Pastor Mark & RealFaith. 68

REAL GROUPS
WITH REALFAITH

Faith that does not result in good deeds is not real faith.
James 2:20, TLB

At RealFaith, we believe that the Word of God isn't just for us to read, it's to be obeyed. And living in community with fellow believers is one of the ways God the Father allows us to learn and grow to become more like His Son Jesus through the power of the Holy Spirit. We do this through something called Real Groups. Here are a few tips to start your own.

1. Invite
Invite your friends, neighbors, family, coworkers, and enemies, because they all need Jesus whether they know Him or not! Whether it's a group of men, women, families, students, or singles, explain that you'd like to start a weekly sermon-based small group based on Pastor Mark Driscoll's sermons.

2. Listen to the sermon on realfaith.com or on the RealFaith app
You can host a viewing party to watch RealFaith Live and discuss it all at once, or you can watch it separately and gather to discuss it at another time that works for the group.

3. Get into God's Word
In addition to watching the sermon, make sure you and all group members have a study guide from realfaith.com for

the current sermon series. There are questions for personal reflection as well as for groups that can guide your devotional times throughout the week. You can also sign up for Daily Devos at **realfaith.com.**

4. Gather together
Whether at someone's house, a public place, or through something like Zoom, meet weekly to discuss the sermon and what God has taught you through it. The great thing about Real Groups is that you don't all have to be in the same location. You can talk about sermon takeaways, what stood out to you in the study guide, or what God taught you in His Word that week. Focus on personal application as much as possible.

5. Pray
When you gather, feel free to share prayer requests, pray for each other on the spot, and continue praying throughout the week. Prayer is a great unifying force that God gives us to strengthen His family.

6. Share
Send us photos, videos, testimonies, and updates of how your group is doing to **hello@realfaith.com**. You might even be featured on our RealFaith Live show!

We will be praying for you and your group and look forward to hearing what God does through it.

CHAPTER 1
Black & White in a Rainbow World

Two of the most iconic and prolific symbols scattered throughout western culture are the cross and the rainbow.

The cross has long served as the symbol of Christian faith, reminding believers in every generation following Jesus' death and resurrection in our place for our sins the depth of our sin and love of our Savior. While the early church embraced several symbols, including the fish and the loaf, the cross symbolized the believer's connection with the death of Jesus. The church father Tertullian (155–230) tells us of the early practice of believers making the sign of the cross over their bodies with their hand and adorning their necks and homes with crosses to celebrate the brutal death of Jesus.

In the Bible, the rainbow is a symbol of God's holiness and divine judgment, just like the cross. In the first book of the Bible, after God flooded the earth in the days of Noah in judgment of constant and unrepentant human sin, God placed a rainbow in the sky as a symbol of the Noahic covenant promise that He would not bring that flood again.[a] In the ancient world, a bow was the weapon of choice for skilled warriors. When a battle was concluded, and the warrior entered into peacetime, they would hang their bow on the wall in their home as a symbol that war had ended. God was doing the same thing hanging the rainbow in the sky. The rainbow also appears in the last book of the Bible,

---

[a] Genesis 9:12-16

surrounding the throne of Jesus Christ ruling and reigning from His throne in the unseen realm while being worshipped by divine beings and departed saints. Revelation 4:3 says, "he who sat there had the appearance of jasper and carnelian, and around the throne was a rainbow..."

Because what God creates Satan counterfeits, today, the rainbow symbol has been stolen and repurposed as a mockery of God and celebration of sin. The rainbow flag, as is currently used throughout culture, especially in June for Pride month, began in 1978. A gay drag queen artist created the now-iconic symbol with hot pink denoting sex, red representing life, yellow reminding of the sun, green pointing to nature, turquoise celebrating art, indigo symbolizing harmony, and violet serving as an ode to the spirit world, which includes the demonic.

Bible-believing Christians think in terms of black and white (binary thinking). Non-Christians think in terms of a spectrum or rainbow. Biblical thinking is binary thinking. Biblical Christianity requires black-and-white thinking because it is dualistic. From beginning to end, the Bible is thoroughly categorical: Satan and God, demons and angels, sin and holiness, lies and truth, wolves and shepherds, non-Christians and Christians, damnation and salvation, Hell and Heaven. An exhaustive list could fill a book—but you get the point. The Bible makes clear distinctions and judgments between opposed categories.

Mainstream culture is monistic. The culture does not allow black-and-white thinking. The culture refuses to allow any categories because that would mean making distinctions, which ultimately ends in making value judgments. Instead of Satan and God, we have a "higher power". Instead of demons and angels, we have spirits or ghosts. Instead of sin and holiness, we have lifestyle choice. Instead of lies and absolute truth, we have your truth and my truth. Instead of wolves and shepherds, we have spiritual guides. Instead of non-Christians and Christians, we have everyone defined as God's children. Instead of damnation and salvation, we have whatever works for you. Instead of Hell and Heaven, we have people who go to a "better place" when they die.

Monism is a religion. Although not always formal like Christianity, it is a religious view of the world that rejects dualistic thinking. Ultimately, if we believe Scripture, this is a battle between the God of the Bible, who is intolerant, and the gods of this world, who are at war against Him.

Learn to Discern

God commands His people to not just come to different conclusions than non-Christians, but to have a completely different mindset.
- Matthew 22:37 – [Jesus] said to him, "You shall love the Lord your God with all your heart and with all your soul and with all your mind…"
- Romans 8:5-7 – For those who live according to the flesh set their minds on the things of the flesh, but those who live according to the Spirit set their minds on the things of the Spirit. For to set the mind on the flesh is death, but to set the mind on the Spirit is life and peace. For the mind that is set on the flesh is hostile to God, for it does not submit to God's law; indeed, it cannot.
- Romans 12:1-2 – I appeal to you therefore, brothers, by the mercies of God, to present your bodies as a living sacrifice, holy and acceptable to God, which is your spiritual worship. Do not be conformed to this world, but be transformed by the renewal of your mind…
- 1 Corinthians 2:16 – "For who has understood the mind of the Lord so as to instruct him?" But we have the mind of Christ…

The believer's ability to judge between truth and lies, good and evil, right and wrong by the aid of the Holy Spirit illuminating the Word of God is generally referred to as "discernment". In the Old Testament (OT), "The key Hebrew word is bîn. It and its derivatives are used some 247 times in the OT and are usually translated "understanding". The basic idea is that of understanding gained by evaluating. Thus, words like "discern," "distinguish," and "judgment" capture the basic meaning of bîn.[1]

Although the concept of discernment appears repeatedly throughout the New Testament (NT), "In the NT "discern" and "discernment" occur only four times. Three of the Greek terms are based on the root krínō (*kritikós, anakrínō, diakrínō*), which basically meant "sift" or "distinguish," then "select" or "divide out," and finally received the common meaning "decide" or (esp in the NT) "judge".[2]

The motive for the writing of Jude is largely discernment. The theme of Jude is found in verse 3, which is a battle cry to, "contend for the faith that was once for all delivered to the saints". This imagery taken from physical war that is applied to spiritual warfare, is that a demonic invasion has occurred in the church as God's people had been infiltrated by the Enemy camp. To "contend" for the heart of the gospel, which is never changing and "delivered" just "once" for all true "saints" in all of Church history are some specific commands that apply to every age and every deception that seeks to dilute the purity of the gospel of Jesus Christ.

One Bible commentary says, "In every age there has prevailed in the Church a proneness to depart both from the principles and practice of the Gospel. St. Jude in his day, writing to the whole Christian Church respecting "their common salvation," says, "it was needful for him to write to them, and to exhort them all to contend earnestly for the faith once delivered to the saints".[3]

Wise, Foolish, Evil

Some of the worst advice we give people, starting when they are young, is to treat everyone the same. The truth is that we should treat different people differently. Not everyone is safe, and dangerous people should not be treated the same as loving, godly, healthy, and safe people. There are three groups of people that Jude distinguishes, and he treats each group very differently, instructing Christians to do the same.

One, the wise people are mature Christians who Jude is encouraging to help act as shepherds, looking after and building up the new and immature Christians. The wise people in the church are called "beloved" four times as people, "kept for Jesus Christ", and recipients of "mercy", which is mentioned four times along with, "peace, and love" from God. With pastoral affection, Jude encourages these believers that they have the "Holy Spirit" who ensures "eternal life" and a blameless eternity in Jesus' Kingdom.

Two, the foolish people are immature (and possibly new Christians) whom Jude is treating as sheep vulnerable to wolves that have invaded the local church flock. The wise people in the church are encouraged to protect these sheep against the wolves and both "have mercy on those who doubt" and "save others by snatching them out of the fire; to others show mercy without fear..."

Three, the evil people are deceptive, dangerous, and divisive apostates as, "Apostasy is the turning away from God in rebellion or apathy. God's people must beware of inward rebelliousness as much as the outward wickedness that manifests such rebellion."[4]

Apostates are not lost people who need Jesus. Apostates are people who profess to be Christians, build relationships with Christians in a church to earn trust and cause division, but do not believe what the Bible teaches or behave how the Bible commands. Because they have relationships with

Christians in a church, often find their way into leadership or teaching roles, and are cunningly deceptive, apostates are particularly dangerous, just like a wolf who gets into a pen with vulnerable sheep. Judas Iscariot serves as a frightening example of an apostate.

The original Greek word for apostasy was derived from treason in battle. A military term, it referred to war when a soldier abandons their nation, betrays their king, and joins the enemy side of the battle. The first apostate was Satan who then recruited angels he was in relationship with to war against God and godliness. In every age, Satan continues this apostasy, seeking to recruit people in churches to join his demons in the battle. This explains why Jude refers to the fall of angels who became demons (5-7); along with Cain-Balaam-Korah who were all apostates either in belief or behavior (11). This apostasy is precisely what is occurring in Jude's day, and our own, as the Bible does not tell us what used to happen, but rather what always happens.

One Bible commentary on the book of Jude summarizes the six marks of apostasy as

1. impiety ("ungodly," vv. 4, 15, 18)
2. arrogance, claiming a false authority ("denied ... Jesus," v. 4; "claim authority," v. 8; "brag loudly about themselves," v. 16) and even "scoff at supernatural beings" (v. 8)
3. immorality ("grace allows us to live immoral lives," v. 4; "live immoral lives," v. 8; "ungodly desires," vv. 16, 18; "follow their natural instincts," v. 19)
4. greed ("deceive people for money," v. 11; "care only for themselves," v. 12; "flatter others to get what they want," v. 16)
5. rebellion ("defy authority," v. 8; "scoff at supernatural beings," v. 8, and at "things they do not understand," v. 10; likened to Korah's rebellion, v. 11)
6. divisiveness ("grumblers and complainers," v. 16;

"insults ... spoken against him," v. 15; "creating divisions among you," v. 19)[5]

Another Bible commentary summarizes the book saying, "The epistle of Jude serves to cultivate faithfulness among true believers who are surrounded by apostasy."[6]

In our day, the tone and tenor of Jude will seem, at first, unloving, intolerant, and judgmental to modern ears. Throughout the Bible, God is referred to as a Father, both for the Church on earth and in Heaven as His house, and Jesus as the door into the Father's house. Any good father knows they need to have a door on their house to protect the people who are part of the family from those who would want to do harm. A good father also warns their children that not everyone is safe, and that they should not automatically open the door to anyone who knocks on it. The entire reason that a good father does not welcome everyone into his house is because he is loving. To be sure, those who are not welcomed into a family's home may feel rejected, outcast, and unwelcome, but it is not so much because the good father hates them, but rather because he lovingly protects his family. Unlike our homes, the Father's house is open to anyone who wants to join the family. They must simply pass by faith through the door of Jesus Christ and agree to obey the Father to live with their spiritual brothers and sisters. In Jude, Jesus' little brother is functioning as the spiritual father warning a local church that the family was in danger, some people did not belong to Jesus, and they were not obeying God the Father, which made them a threat to be dealt with.

Getting Vertical

Over the Church universally, and churches locally like the one Jude writes to, is God. Throughout Jude, the entire Trinity appears. At the beginning of the letter, "God the Father" is mentioned. The Son of God is referred to as "Jesus Christ" twice, "Jesus" once, "our Lord Jesus Christ", and "the only God, our Savior, through Jesus Christ our Lord." On one occasion, "the Holy Spirit" is also mentioned as the power in our prayer and living in the love of God.

Jude keeps pointing believers up to God ruling and reigning over all the nonsense in culture that seeks to corrupt and compromise the church like a cancer. A doxology (taken from the ancient Greek word referring to a song or praise, honor, and glory) closes the book with an epic glorifying of God in triumph, "Now to him who is able to keep you from stumbling and to present you blameless before the presence of his glory with great joy, to the only God, our Savior, through Jesus Christ our Lord, be glory, majesty, dominion, and authority, before all time and now and forever. Amen."

In our day, like the days of Jude, there is generational apostasy commonly referred to as "wokeism". Hard woke churches are, tragically, surrendering to a spiritual invasion from false teaching wolves on everything from gender to marriage, sexuality, and the embracing of beliefs and behaviors that are celebrated in parades but should be repented of by God's people. As Jude exhorts, God's people in every age need to "contend" for the unchanging truths of God's Word. To do that, we need to get vertical, find God in glory as the true north on the compass of our soul, and spend much time in prayer and worship, going up to God to gain discernment about the spiritual war that rages around us.

CHAPTER 2
10 Fun Facts from Jude

Can you imagine what it would have been like to grow up with Jesus Christ as your big brother? When we read the Bible and learn about Mary and Joseph, it is hard to imagine that they were Jude's parents. In reading the book of James, it's intriguing to consider that Mary and Joseph's sons included God incarnate and pastors who penned books of the Bible bearing their names. These three boys possibly shared a bunk bed, spent their days fishing as kids, and threw the ball around the yard.

The fact that Jesus' family, all devoutly Jewish believers, worshipped Jesus as their only God and Savior is a compelling argument that Jesus rose from the dead to prove His claims to be God. His family members all believed that worshipping the wrong God would doom a person to eternal torment in Hell as an enemy of God. Had Christ stayed dead, Christians would have not risen up, starting with Jesus' family.

Before we begin studying Jude's brief book of the Bible, there are some fun facts that make his work unique. We will examine 10 of them before studying the book in verse-by-verse fashion.

One, there are numerous people named Jude in the New Testament. A Bible commentary says, "Jude was a common name. It was first borne by Judah, the son of Jacob and head of the tribe of Judah. The tribal head Judah is listed in Jesus' genealogy (Matt. 1:2–3; Luke 3:33); references to the name and the land of his tribe occur frequently (Matt. 2:6; Luke 2:4; Heb. 7:14; Rev. 5:5; 7:5). The designation *Jude* is the English variant of 'Judas.' In English we distinguish Jude, the writer of the epistle, from Judas Iscariot, who betrayed Jesus. However, other persons mentioned in the New Testament have the name *Judas*:

1. Judas, the son of James (Luke 6:16; Acts 1:13). He was one of the twelve disciples. He is also known as Thaddeus (compare Matt. 10:3; Mark 3:18; also see John 14:22).
2. Judas the Galilean (Acts 5:37). He was a revolutionary who was killed because of his subversive activities.
3. Judas Barsabbas, who was present at the Jerusalem Council and served as letter carrier to the Gentile churches (Acts 15:22, 27, 32).
4. Judas, an ancestor of Jesus (Luke 3:33; see also v. 30).
5. Judas, the brother of James and the (half) brother of Jesus (Matt. 13:55; Mark 6:3).[7]

It is the last Jude, Jesus' half-brother, who is the author of the book bearing his name. Jude 1 speaks of, "Jude, a servant of Jesus Christ and brother of James..."

If you were raised Catholic, as I was, you may have wrongly been taught that Mary remained a virgin throughout her life and that Jesus had no siblings. Arguments for the perpetual virginity of Mary arose as early as the second century, became more popular in the fourth century, and culminated with the Second Council of Constantinople, which convened in 553 and declared Mary "ever virgin". Some early church fathers (e.g., Origen), some Catholic and Protestant theologians (such as Luther, Calvin, Zwingli, and Wesley), the Second Helvetic Confession and the Geneva Bible say that Mary was "ever virgin," or *semper virgo*. This teaching is inaccurate for multiple reasons. God designed marriage to include physical union and said that depriving marital intimacy is a sin.ᵃ Matthew 1:25 says that they did have relations following Jesus' birth: "But [he] knew her not until she had given birth to a son." Scripture also repeatedly states that Mary had other sons and daughters, which we will examine next.

Two, Jesus' half-brother Jude is mentioned multiple times in the New Testament:

- Matthew 12:46–50 (cf. Mark 3:31-35; Luke 8:19–21) – While he [Jesus] was still speaking to the people, behold, his mother and his brothers stood outside, asking to speak to him. But he replied to the man who told him, "Who is my mother, and who are my brothers?" And stretching out his hand toward his disciples, he said, "Here are my mother and my brothers! For whoever does the will of my Father in heaven is my brother and sister and mother."
- Matthew 13:55–56 – "…Is not this the carpenter's son? Is not his mother called Mary? And are not his brothers James and Joseph and Simon and Judas? And are not all his sisters with us? Where then did this man get all these things?"
- Mark 6:3 – "…Is not this the carpenter, the son of Mary and brother of James and Joses and Judas and Simon? And are not his sisters here with us?" And they took offense at him.
- John 2:12 – After this he [Jesus] went down to Capernaum, with his mother and his brothers and his disciples, and they stayed there for a few days.
- Acts 1:14 – All these with one accord were devoting themselves to prayer, together with the women and Mary the mother of Jesus, and his brothers.
- 1 Corinthians 9:5 – Do we not have the right to take

ᵃ 1 Cor. 7:3-5

along a believing wife, as do the other apostles and the brothers of the Lord and Cephas?
- Jude 1 – Jude, a servant of Jesus Christ and brother of James...

Three, Jude is one of the shortest books of the New Testament (2-3 John are the shortest). At just 25 verses, it takes up just one printed page in many Bibles.

Four, Jude is among the most neglected and seldom studied or preached books of the New Testament. One Bible scholar says of it, "The most neglected book in the New Testament is probably the book of Jude."[8] Another Bible commentator says, "Jude is largely unknown and seldom read."[9] Despite not getting the attention it deserves, Jude is a timeless and therefore timely "fiery cross to rouse the churches".[10]

Puritan Bible commentator Matthew Henry says Jude, "is designed to warn us against seducers and their seduction, to inspire us with a warm love to, and a hearty concern for, truth (evident and important truth), and that in the closest conjunction with holiness, of which charity, or sincere unbiased brotherly-love, is a most essential character and inseparable branch. The truth we are to hold fast, and endeavour that others may be acquainted with and not depart from."[11]

Five, Jude quotes a handful of ancient sources outside of the Bible. Jude quotes *1 Enoch*, and alludes to the *Assumption of Moses* (4,6,7,9,12,14-15). Some understandably wonder how a perfect book written by the Holy Spirit through Jude could quote imperfect books not written by the Holy Spirit. The Bible itself models the fact that there is at least some truth outside of the Bible. The Old Testament occasionally quotes other books, such as the *Book of Jashar* and the *Book of the Wars of the Lord*.[a] In the

---
[a] Josh. 10:13; 2 Sam. 1:18; Num. 21:14

New Testament, Paul quotes a pagan poet[a], as well as well as a non-canonical book outside of the Bible.[b] In quoting these sources outside Scripture, the Bible is not saying that they should be included as sacred Scripture but rather that they do contain some truth. Likewise, a mechanic, doctor, or computer programmer does not have to consult Leviticus to turn a brake drum, perform open-heart surgery, or make an addition to a software program.

Six, Jude uses a lot of Old Testament examples of apostasy. One Bible commentary says, "Egypt, Sodom and Gomorrah, Moses, Cain, Balaam, Korah, Enoch, Adam, and the fallen angels all point to a people familiar with Old Testament history and possibly apocryphal literature."[12]

Seven, as is common in ancient Jewish writing, Jude makes points in poetic ways. A Bible Commentary says, "notice these other repetitive patterns, some triplets and some longer:
- Called—loved—kept (v. 1)
- Grace—mercy—love (v. 2)
- Pollute—reject—slander (v. 8)
- Clouds—trees—waves—stars (vv. 12–13)
- Ungodly—ungodly—ungodly (v. 15)
- Divide—follow—without the Spirit (v. 19)
- Be merciful—save—show mercy (vv. 22–23)"[13]

Eight, there are numerous similarities between Jude and the New Testament book of 2 Peter.
- Jude 4 echoes 2 Peter 2:1,3
- Jude 6 echoes 2 Peter 2:4
- Jude 7 echoes 2 Peter 2:6
- Jude 8 echoes 2 Peter 2:10
- Jude 9 echoes 2 Peter 2:11
- Jude 10 echoes 2 Peter 2:12
- Jude 11 echoes 2 Peter 2:15

---

[a] Acts 17:28 [b] 2 Tim. 3:8

- Jude 12 echoes 2 Peter 2:13,17
- Jude 13 echoes 2 Peter 2:18
- Jude 16 echoes 2 Peter 2:18
- Jude 17-18 echoes 2 Peter 3:2-3

Nine, there are numerous actions that Jude commands God's people take to keep themselves in right relationship with God and one another:

- "Contend" – the language here is of having healthy conflict, standing up to false teachers and evildoers, and calling heresy on anyone who encourages tolerance of sin (especially sexual sin) instead of repentance of sin.
- "Remind" – Christians are prone to forget things they have learned, and so we must remind one another of the truths that we have learned in the past but need to apply in the present. Often, a time of spiritual war does not require new teaching but instead a new commitment to obey timeless truths.
- "Remember" – Jude quotes the New Testament teachings of Jesus and the Apostles to remind us that we must never forget that the Word of God is the truest truth and the place we must constantly return. The Bible is referred to as a "sword" for spiritual battle and God's people need to wield it wisely.
- "Build yourselves up" – like a soldier will train their body for physical war, a Christian must train their soul for spiritual war. Healthy habits like Bible reading, prayer, corporate worship, healthy Christian relationships, repenting of sin, serving, and giving are how this happens.
- "Pray in the Holy Spirit" – the Holy Spirit in a believer teaches them how to pray to the Lord so that they can be unburdened, get clarity on God's will for their life, grow in discernment between good and evil, and be empowered to live for God in a hostile world.

- "Keep yourselves in the love of God" – like any relationship, we can drift from the close intimacy with and enjoyment of the Lord and need to always make this our highest priority.
- "Waiting for the mercy of our Lord Jesus Christ that leads to eternal life" – we need mercy to get us through this life, with God not giving us what we deserve through sin, and it is mercy that allows us to live in love with others and look forward to the eternal mercy awaiting all of God's children forever.
- "Have mercy on those who doubt" and "show mercy without fear" – some people are not corrupt, but rather confused and need God's people in relationship with them to give them mercy, love, and help to come to a healthier spiritual state.
- "Save others by snatching them out of the fire" – some people have been deceived and led astray by such things as an ungodly relationship, false teaching, financial gain, or pleasure (often sexual) that has seduced them from walking with God faithfully. If we are in relationship with such people, we need to act like a firefighter and do all we can to get them away from the flames that will consume them.

Ten, Jude is easy to read, and you should read it every day while you are utilizing this study guide as it only takes 5-10 minutes and is packed with intense imagery the Holy Spirit will bring to mind in the years to come as you need it. The early church father Origen says, "In its own right, Jude is a remarkable piece of literature. Rich and original in style and vocabulary, this short letter is "filled with flowing words of heavenly grace".[14]

BLACK & WHITE IN A RAINBOW WORLD

CHAPTER 3
11 Warnings Before Studying Jude

When a wild animal is caught, before it can be domesticated, it has to undergo what is called a "cage phase". During this time, the beast is so wild that, if it is not constrained, it will ferociously maim and even kill.

When you start learning the Bible, along with some of the debates throughout church history up to the present, it is common to either enter into a "cage phase" or run into some folks who are in it themselves. Cage phase Christians are prone to constantly being triggered by most any teaching or conversation, quickly get heated, stay on the offensive which makes others defensive, paint issues with a broad brush, and win a lot of arguments while losing a lot of relationships. Some Christians spend their entire life in the "cage phase", and some Christian groups pride themselves on acting like jihadists for Jesus, blowing things up and setting things on fire whenever possible.

Cage phase Christianity is not discernment but rather a destructive disservice. To help you be discerning, it will help to consider what discernment is not so you can more clearly understand what it is. The following 11 warnings come from practical experience in my own life as a zealous young Christian who was guilty of many of these warnings, and as a pastor for three decades who has had a front row seat to every one of these shortcomings that are, sadly, common and create unnecessary division between God's people.

1. **Choose faith over fear.** When we learn about wolves, false teachers, and apostasy all empowered by demonic forces, it can cause some people to become fearful. If fear is a dominating oppression in your mind and over your life, it can lead to paranoia. The opposite of fear is faith that God is over all evil and is faithful to give you discernment to live the life He has created you for and called you to.

2. **Choose humility over pride.** People who begin to get a bit of knowledge about theology and doctrine, including various heresies throughout Church history, can fall into the same trap as the Devil, and be puffed up with knowledge instead of filled up with love as Paul warns. The goal of learning is not to show how smart you are or how dumb someone else is. The goal of learning is to hear from God and help others do the same so that you can humbly live in obedience.

3. **Choose a teachable spirit over a critical spirit.** Some people who are the most critical, judgmental, self-righteous, and divisive will say that they are called to a ministry of discernment and holding complete strangers accountable (usually by forming an angry mob of strangers online to commence with the handing out of pitchforks, flaming torches, and dead cats to fling). People with a critical spirit assume that anyone who disagrees with them disagrees with God. Why? Because they think they have every answer to every question and nothing more to learn. The result is that when a person with a critical spirit hears or reads something, they are not looking for what they can learn, but only what they can attack, criticize, or correct, because they are always the teacher grading the paper and never the student taking the test.

4. **Choose facts over myths.** If we've learned anything in

recent years as the Internet has overtaken the world, it is that there are lots of lies and misinformation that are presented as truth and facts. As a more public person than most, I have just accepted that much if not most of what is said about me is largely or entirely untrue. To be discerning is to get the facts and not surrender to speculation. As the famed Baptist preacher Charles Spurgeon once quipped, it seems like a lie can run around the world before the truth can even get its shoes on.

5. **Choose to use Jude as a mirror before using it as binoculars.** Religious people use the Bible as binoculars to judge and even condemn others. Repentant people first use the Bible as a mirror to judge themselves before using it as binoculars to judge others. As you study Jude (and the rest of the Bible), seek what needs to change in your beliefs and behaviors before you do the same for other people.

6. **Choose to make what you are for a higher priority than what you are against.** To be sure, because some people and things are "anti-Christ", we have to be against those people and things. However, if we are known only for who or what we are against, rather than Jesus and life in the Spirit, which we are for, we are falling short of true gospel ministry. Beware of those bloggers, YouTubers, and social media influencers who make their living on attacking by beating people down, not discipling to build people up.

7. **Choose to critique ideas more frequently than individuals.** The New Testament critiques a long list of ideas and a short list of named individuals. As a general rule, the authors of the New Testament only name apostate false teachers and wolves when they are writing to a local church where those people are present, well-known, and causing

great harm.[a] Since you are not a writer of the Bible, and most of the people who are false teachers do not attend your church, it is not your job to hold them accountable. The Lord and local church leaders have that job covered.

8. **Choose to avoid putting everything in the closed hand or open hand.** There are two ways to become apostate in your beliefs. The first is called legalism. Legalism happens when you take issues that should be in the open hand that Bible-believing faithful Christians have always disagreed about (e.g. Bible translation, mode of baptism, age of the earth, speaking in tongues, women as pastors, whether Noah's flood was global or local, when Jesus will return, form of worship music, predestination versus free will, etc.) and placing them in the closed hand, calling anyone who disagrees with your narrow position a heretic or false teacher. The second is called lawlessness. Lawlessness happens when you take issues that should be in the closed hand that faithful Bible-believing Christians have always agreed about and place them in the open hand (e.g. there are only two genders - male and female, marriage is only for one man and one woman, sex is only for heterosexual monogamous marriage, life is sacred and the taking of the life of a child born or unborn is murder, the Bible is the perfect Word of God, Jesus Christ is God, Jesus Christ is the only Savior and way to Heaven, everyone is a sinner by nature and choice and needs Jesus Christ to be saved, etc.) in the false name of tolerance, love, and diversity, which welcomes everyone but God and everything but the Word of God.

9. **Choose to understand the difference between**

---

[a] e.g., Hymenaeus and those who work with him like Alexander, Philetus (1 Timothy 1:18-20; 2 Timothy 2:17-18)

principles and methods. The Bible is filled with principles that God's people in various cultures throughout history under the guidance of godly human leadership and the Holy Spirit are free (within reason) to apply with varying methods. For example, a local Christian church is supposed to gather, but this can happen in a home, at a rented movie theater, in a majestic cathedral, or under a tree in the wilderness. Christians are told to worship the Lord, but what songs they sing, instruments they use (if any), and language they utilize varies greatly. Some people wrongly confuse principles and methods, so that if you are not using their method then you are guilty of violating God's principle, which is often untrue. We have unity in our biblical principles, and diversity in our methods.

10. **Choose to give grace, not law, to the right people.** New Christians, prodigals who have returned to the Lord, and those who have little or bad Bible teaching often say things that are similar to apostates. The Bible encourages us to look at people's hearts, and such people love the Lord in their heart but have a lot of things to learn about Him in their mind. Rather than going on the offensive against these people as you would a heretic, choose to help them learn and grow as Jude 22-23 commands, "have mercy on those who doubt; save others by snatching them out of the fire; to others show mercy with fear..."

11. **Choose to be healthy, not unhealthy.** The New Testament often exhorts God's people to have "sound doctrine"[a], also called, "sound words"[b], "sound speech"[c], "sound teaching"[d], or "sound faith"[e]. The original Greek word translated "sound" can also be rightly translated as the

---

[a] 1 Timothy 1:10; Titus 1:9, 2:1 [b] 1 Timothy 6:3; 2 Timothy 1:13 [c] Titus 2:8 [d] 2 Timothy 4:3 [e] Titus 1:13, 2:2

English word "healthy". Just as a sound diet helps a person be physically healthy, so too sound Bible teaching helps a person be spiritually healthy. The goal of the Bible is not just to fill our heads with information, but to fill all of who we are, what we believe, and how we behave with transformation. Sadly, some people weaponize the Bible to wrongly defend themselves, wrongly attack others, and wrongly cause division and pain among God's people. This behavior is often done in the name of fighting for sound doctrine, but it is not healthy and therefore it does not live up to its own defining and defending. Sound doctrine makes someone more aware of the goodness of God, badness of their sin, increases their love for Jesus as their Savior and Lord, gives them compassion for hurting and lost people, and motivates them to give and serve out of love as God has loved them by yielding to the Holy Spirit at work in and through them.

As a general rule, the principle of innocent until proven guilty is a good one to apply when meeting and getting to know people who claim to be Christians. Most professing Christians are not heretics or apostates, although there are some, and those who are teachers and leaders are very dangerous. Most professing Christians haven't been taught a lot, are struggling with life issues like the rest of us, and could use a loving hand up that isn't shaped like a fist. The first is reserved for the faithless few who are willful and intentional apostate heretics who live more like Judas than Jesus. Having established the difference between being discerning and critical, we will now jump in and begin studying Jude verse-by-verse.

CHAPTER 4
Jude Personal and Group Study Guide

In boating, the goal is to have the boat in the water, but not let the water enter into the boat. If you are in a boat at sea, and it starts to take on water, you know you have a crisis on your hands.

The world is a bit like a tumultuous ocean, and the Church is supposed to be like a boat passing through that sea picking up people who are adrift and rescuing them by pulling them into the boat. When the world starts to flood into the church, there is a crisis.

This is precisely the backdrop for the book of Jude. Having watched his big brother, Jesus Christ, die for sinners, raise from death, and return to Heaven, Jude was part of the first days of the early church. Some years later, the zeal of the first Christians began to wane, and new generations of Christians were starting to fill the church up with the world, which created a crisis that threatened to sink the Christian Church altogether.

If you can image a crew on a boat at sea many miles away from the shore bailing water and patching holes, frantically hoping to prevent the brutal death of everyone onboard, then you can imagine the backdrop for the sense of urgency that Jude writes with. The same worldly waters that were leaking into the ark of the church in Jude's day continue to leak into the Church in our day – prideful rejection of godly authority, spirituality without the Holy Spirit, and sexual sin of every sort propelled by gender confusion and a celebration of pleasure in most any and every form.

To help you navigate the stormy seas in our day, we will study the book of Jude verse-by-verse. The timeless truths in Jude are exactly what we need in our truthless times.

Week 1: Are You a Real Christian?

Scripture to Read: Jude 1-2

Scripture for Memorization and Meditation:
Jude 1-2 – Jude, a servant of Jesus Christ and brother of James, To those who are called, beloved in God the Father and kept for Jesus Christ: May mercy, peace, and love be multiplied to you.

Commentary:

If you become a Christian later in life and don't have much experience with Christian churches, trying to pick a good church can be very complicated. As a new Christian in college, for example, I was wary of joining any church because I did not know the differences between the various Christian denominations, or the differing theological ways of interpreting parts of the Bible. Even more concerning was the thought of accidentally joining a cult that pretended to be Christian and getting sucked into a nightmare situation. Thankfully, the Holy Spirit led me to a wonderful Bible-teaching, Jesus-loving, joyful church family to begin my journey with Jesus as a new Christian.

How do we know if we are a real Christian and who the real Christians are versus the fake Christians? In every age, from the days of Jesus and Jude to our own, this has been a heated question with warring opinions.

The word "Christian" first appeared in the Bible in Acts 11:26. A Bible dictionary says, "The word 'Christian' (Χριστιανός, Christianos) is a Latinized adjectival derivation of 'Christ' (Χριστό, Christos), denoting intimate relation to Jesus. The earliest usage of the term 'Christian' to denote a follower of Jesus..."[15]

The reason that there are false Christians is two-fold. One, the real God is Creator, and Satan is counterfeiter.

Two, just as the real God is Jesus Christ, Satan also has numerous counterfeits of Christ. In 2 Corinthians 11:3–4, Paul says, "I am afraid that as the serpent deceived Eve by his cunning, your thoughts will be led astray from a sincere and pure devotion to Christ. For if someone comes and proclaims another Jesus than the one we proclaimed, or if you receive a different spirit from the one you received, or if you accept a different gospel from the one you accepted, you put up with it readily enough."

Throughout history, counterfeit Christs have been on the rise, including in our own day, as I co-wrote about many years ago in a book called *Vintage Jesus*. Progressive woke "Christians" say Jesus was merely a good man, but they are not clear about His being the God-man. Jehovah's Witnesses say that Jesus was merely Michael the archangel, a created being that became a man. Mormonism teaches that Jesus was not God but only a man who became one of many gods; it furthermore teaches that he was a polygamist and a half-brother of Lucifer. Unitarian Universalism teaches that Jesus was not God but rather a great man to be respected solely for his teaching, love, justice, and healing. New Age guru Deepak Chopra told Larry King, "I see Christ as a state of consciousness we can all aspire to."[16] According to Scientology, Jesus is an "implant" forced upon a Thetan about a million years ago. Bahá'ís say that Jesus was a manifestation of God and a prophet but inferior to Muhammad and Bahá'u'lláh. Buddhism teaches that Jesus was not God but rather an enlightened man like the Buddha. Hinduism, with its many views of Jesus, does not consider Him to be the only God, but most likely a wise man or incarnation of God much like Krishna. Islam teaches that Jesus was merely a man and a prophet who is inferior to Muhammad. The Dalai Lama said, "[Jesus] was either a fully enlightened being, or a bodhisvatta [a being who aids others to enlightenment] of a very high spiritual realization."[17]

Indian Hindu leader Mahatma Gandhi said, "I cannot ascribe exclusive divinity to Jesus. He is as divine as Krishna or Rama or Muhammad or Zoroaster."[18]

Before we can discern who the real Christians are, we must discern who the real Christ is. Who knew Jesus best? Obviously, His family. No one knows us as well as our family. They see the true you, when no one else is watching, and if anyone would have known that Jesus was not born of a virgin, sinless, and risen from death to prove His claims to be God, it would be Jesus' family.

In another book called *Spirit-Filled Jesus*, I explain this saying, "Beyond a few of their names, we know very little about Jesus' brothers and sisters except for His half-brothers James and Jude. Although he was Jesus' brother (Matt. 13:55), James was not a believer until Jesus appeared to him following the resurrection (Mark 3:21; 1 Cor. 15:7). He was with the apostles at Pentecost (Acts 1:14) and became a leader of the Jerusalem church (Gal. 1:19, 2:9; Acts 12:17, 15:12–21). His two nicknames are 'James the Just' for his character and 'Camel Knees' from praying so much."

In Jude 1, the author introduces himself as, "Jude, a servant of Jesus Christ and brother of James..." In Galatians 2:9, Paul calls James a pillar holding up the church along with Cephas (Peter) and John. Both James and Jude went on to be devoted Christian pastors, worshipping their big brother Jesus and writing books of the Bible bearing their names. James also presided over the conference held in Jerusalem to welcome Gentile converts in the church.[a] His work opened up the gospel beyond the Jewish people and can be credited in large part for the existence of Christianity as a global movement of the Spirit to this day. Additionally, James died a martyr's death in service to his half-brother. We read that, "...James the half-brother of Jesus was executed...

---

[a] Acts 15

he was thrown off the temple and still alive, was stoned to death."[19] Dying, James echoed His big brother Jesus from Luke 23:34 saying, "...forgive them, for they know not what they do."[20] One archaeological expert says, "When James is murdered...it is Simon...who takes over leadership of the movement."[21]

Jesus' Spirit-filled family is the most incredible and impactful for good in world history. Before Jesus died and rose, His family (including his half-brothers James and Jude) thought he had lost His mind claiming to be God come down from Heaven to die on the cross and rise from the dead to save sinners.[a] Everything changed when Jude and the rest of Jesus' family (along with His friends and followers) saw our Lord physically risen from death and ascended into Heaven, which causes His "mother" and "brothers" to begin worshipping Him as God as the first members of the early church.[b] One Bible commentary says, "Though others called Jude 'brother of the Lord' (1 Cor. 9:5), he preferred to style himself *brother of James and servant of Jesus Christ*. It is a further mark of his modesty that he was prepared to accept the position of playing second fiddle to James, his more celebrated brother. Barclay cites the parallel of Andrew, content to be known as Simon Peter's brother. 'Both Jude and Andrew might well have been jealous and resentful of their far greater brothers. Both must have had the gift of gladly taking second place.'"[22]

Once we have the real Christ, we can then determine if we are really a Christian, and who the real Christians are. In the opening lines of Jude, we learn that true Christians follow Christ by remaining under godly authority because they are:

1. Called by God into a saving relationship through Jesus Christ
2. Beloved by God as His adoptive child

---

[a] John 7:5; Mark 3:21,31 [b] Acts 1:14

3. Kept by God so that salvation cannot be lost because God does not lose a Christian
4. Recipients of ever-multiplying mercy from God, peace with God, and love to share with others, starting with fellow believers.

Lastly, although Jude is Jesus' brother, he simply refers to himself as "a servant of Jesus Christ". A Bible commentary says, "It has an overtone of great importance, for Abraham, Moses, David and Daniel are all called 'servants of God'."[24]

Becoming a Christian meant that Jesus went from being Jude's brother to his Savior and Lord. Simply knowing Jesus in a close, loving relationship was not enough, Jude needed to repent of sin and trust in Jesus as His God and Savior. Many people who grow up in the church are like Jude – they know a lot about Jesus and are friendly toward Him but have not yet been saved by Him.

Dig Deeper.
1. Begin reading Jude once a day for all the weeks you are studying this great book of the Bible (it takes 5-10 minutes).
2. Jude calls himself, "a servant of Jesus Christ". Look up what the Bible has to say about being a servant like Jesus Christ (Matthew 20:20-28, 23:1-12; John 13:12-17; Philippians 2:1-11).
3. Jude was Jesus' brother. Look up what the Bible says about being adopted into God's family with Jesus as your new Big Brother (Matthew 12:46-50; Romans 8:14-16; Galatians 4:4-7).

Walk it out. Talk it out.
1. What is the most encouraging word or phrase that jumps out to you in the opening lines of Jude? Why is that significant to you?
2. What do you think it was like growing up with Jesus

as your big brother, James as your brother, and Mary and Joseph as your parents?
3. When you get to Heaven, if you could ask Jude a question what would it be?
4. How can the group be praying for you?

NOTES

A STUDY IN JUDE

Week 2: Are You a Fake Christian?

Scripture to Read: Jude 3-4

Scripture for Memorization and Meditation:
Jude 3 – ...contend for the faith that was once for all delivered to the saints.

Commentary:
Maintaining physical health is hard work. Keeping up with routine maintenance on your home is a never-ending pursuit. Getting your job done every day at work is a constant struggle. In life, you quickly learn that everything will atrophy, decline, and fall apart unless you intentionally work to maintain it.

What is true physically is also true spiritually. Like gravity that pulls everything south toward Hell, the proclivity in the life of both individual Christians, and local Christian churches, is toward moving in the direction of compromise that leads to corruption and eventually collapse. When fake "Christians" compromise, they're likely perverting the grace of God into a celebration of sexual sin, gender confusion, and rebellion against the sexual biblical guardrails put in place by our "Master and Lord, Jesus Christ".

The theme of Jude is found in the one word, "contend". An academic study of the original Greek word explains that it means, "to exert intense effort...When used in athletic imagery...[it refers to] the one against whom one is contending...the effort expended by the subject in a noble cause...[and the] ideal of dedication to the welfare of the larger group."[25]

A Bible commentary goes on to explain that the word contend "was commonly used in connection with the Greek stadium to denote a strenuous struggle to overcome an opponent, as in a wrestling match. It was also used more generally of any conflict, contest, debate, or lawsuit. Involved is the thought of the expenditure of all one's energy in order to prevail. Here, as often, the verb is used metaphorically to denote a spiritual conflict in which believers are engaged."[26] Another Bible commentary says, "the force of the compound verb as 'to fight, standing upon a thing which is assaulted and which the adversary desires to take away, and it is to fight so as to defend it, and to retain it.'"[27]

    This language of spiritual warfare, with Christians constantly needing to fight against worldly cultural forces seeking to invade and implode the church, requires a vigilance that does not take a season off or ever surrender. Every day, the Enemy of God and His people will be on the attack in everything from lying false teachers to compromised church members who live for tolerance of sin rather than repentance of sin and lip service to Christian faith but who have little interest in truly Christian lifestyle. There is no such thing as stasis in the Christian life. Every day, we are going forward or backward in our walk with Jesus. One Christian academic journal speaks of the reality meant by "contend" in Jude saying, "The present tense indicates that such a defense of the faith is a continuing duty for believers."[28]

    Jude uses very strong language to denounce these apostate wolves with words of war saying, "certain people have crept in unnoticed who long ago were designated for this condemnation, ungodly people, who pervert the grace of our God into sensuality and deny our only Master and Lord, Jesus Christ." Like the evildoers of the Old Testament, they will be "destroyed" because "they "did not believe". Their hellish fate is, "eternal chains under gloomy darkness until the judgment of the great day – just as Sodom and Gomorrah". Because of their "sexual immorality", having "pursued unnatural desire", their fate is "a punishment of eternal fire". In demonic delusion, "these people also, relying on their dreams, defile the flesh, reject authority, and blaspheme the glorious ones". Because "these people blaspheme", they will be "destroyed" for acting like, "unreasoning animals". With a curse, Jude says, "Woe to them! For they walked in the way of Cain and abandoned themselves for the sake of gain...These are blemishes...as they feast with you without fear, looking after themselves; waterless clouds, swept along by winds; fruitless trees in late autumn, twice dead, uprooted; wild waves of the sea, casting up the foam of their own shame; wandering stars, for whom the gloom of utter darkness has been reserved forever." Facing "judgment", these "ungodly" people have "deeds of ungodliness" acting in an "ungodly way" as "ungodly sinners" having said and done "harsh things". Pulling no punches Jude adds, "These are grumblers, malcontents, following their own sinful desires; they are loud-mouthed boasters showing favoritism to gain advantage." These "scoffers, following their ungodly passions...cause divisions, worldly people devoid of the Spirit".

A Bible commentary explains, "He [Jude] wrote to 'exhort' them (Jude 3). In the Greek language, this word was used to describe a general giving orders to the army; hence the atmosphere of this letter is 'military.' Jude had started to write a quiet devotional letter about salvation, but the Spirit led him to put down his harp and sound the trumpet! The Epistle of Jude is a call to arms."[29]

When Jude admonishes Christians to, "contend for the faith that was once for all delivered to the saints", he is referring to a fixed teaching about the gospel of Jesus Christ that is unchanging. The gospel of Jesus Christ is about repentance of sin and faith in his sinless life, substitutionary death, bodily resurrection, rule over all our life as Lord, and coming again to judge the living and the dead with sentencing to Heaven or Hell forever. The gospel has the power of God, and to divert from the gospel, or to dilute the gospel, is to dishonor God and diminish good for people. No generation has the right to make any edits to the Word of God, and every generation will be judged by how faithful they were to hand off what has been handed to them as the body of teaching Christians with the Spirit have held to in every generation of the Church of Jesus Christ.

Dig Deeper.
1. Look up the following Scriptures that give further insights on what it means to "contend" for the faith (1 Peter 3:8-18; 2 Corinthians 10:1-6).
2. Look up the following Scriptures to learn to discern between good and evil so you can contend for your faith (Isaiah 5:20; Romans 12:9, 12:21, 14:16; Hebrews 5:14).
3. Jude calls believers "beloved" here for the first time. Look up the other occasions in the book that also call God's children "beloved" (17,20).
4. Jude calls Christians "saints", which means God sees us not based upon our sin but rather our Savior and His righteousness He has given to us. Read Ephesians 1 to learn more about your identity as a "saint" if you are a Christian.

Walk it out. Talk it out.
1. If you were to explain to a new Christian how to discern the difference between good and evil, how would you explain it?
2. What are some of the issues that are most important for Christians to "contend" for in our day to safeguard God's Word as the highest authority in the Church?
3. In what area of your life is contending for, or standing up for, your Christian beliefs the most difficult (e.g., at work, with family or friends, online, at school, at church, etc.). Why?

4. Is there anyone or anything the group can be praying for you about?

NOTES

A STUDY IN JUDE

Week 3: Are You a Woke Christian?

Scripture to Read: Jude 5-10

Scripture for Memorization and Meditation:
Jude 7 – ...Sodom and Gomorrah and the surrounding cities, which likewise indulged in sexual immorality and pursued unnatural desire, serve as an example by undergoing a punishment of eternal fire.

Commentary:

Today, the term "woke" generally refers to a counterfeit of being born again. To be "woke" purportedly means to be awakened to new perspectives on what is true and false, right and wrong, moral and immoral. Cultural progressives pushing a woke agenda seek to celebrate Pride month as an advancement in gender and sexuality beyond what they would consider repressive traditional male-female sexuality solely within heterosexual marriage, rebel against authority (e.g. God, the Bible, parents, teachers, police officers, etc.), and often profess to be spiritual, if not even a new kind of enlightened Christian marked by tolerance rather than repentance of sin, and love for everything including what God hates.

Some Christians are positive people and have a difficult time saying negative things. Jude is not one of those people. Jude is blistering in his negative critique of false believers who have invaded the church and were encouraging beliefs and behaviors that were against God's Word. Bold, organized, arrogant, and rebellious towards authority, these people threatened the very existence of true Christianity. To show that every generation of true believers has false believers that need to be exposed and rejected, Jude uses multiple negative examples in what might be the most negative book of the New Testament.

Jude's first negative example is taken from the days of Moses in Egypt as recorded in the book of Exodus. After being enslaved, we are told that God rescued a people who lived in freedom, until they died to enter eternal bondage. Jude's big idea is that even if God is doing good things in our life, unless we repent of sin and trust in Him, we will die and suffer eternal misery, having ignored our salvation opportunity.

Jude's second negative example is taken from angels who were created by God as ministers and messengers for Him, and those angels who sinfully rebelled against God and became demons. Unlike human beings, for them, there is no chance of salvation and all that awaits them is "eternal chains under gloomy darkness" and the "judgment of the great day" when everyone is sentenced to Heaven or Hell. Jude also mentions angelic humility in contrast to demonic pride regarding the death of Moses.[a]

Jude's third negative example is Sodom and Gomorrah from Genesis. Apparently, the apostasy in Jude's day is the same as our own. He speaks of "sexual immorality" which refers to sexual sin of any kind, and "unnatural desire" which is a reference to homosexuality. Romans 1:18-32 further builds on the concept and speaks clearly against same sex relations between men and women as "unnatural".

How to interpret why God eviscerated Sodom and Gomorrah with the equivalent of a nuclear strike of fire and flaming road tar from Heaven is hotly debated. For starters, like most sinners, these sinners were guilt of multiple sins. Ezekiel 16:49–50 says, "Behold, this was the guilt of... Sodom...pride, excess of food, and prosperous ease, but did not aid the poor and needy. They were haughty and did an abomination before me. So I removed them, when I saw it." There are six reasons why at least one of the primary

---

[a] Deuteronomy 34:5-6

reasons God killed everyone but one family in Sodom and Gomorrah is for sexual sin, as the men wanted to gang rape what they perceived to be men (but were angels) visiting the city:
1. The sexual sin of Sodom and Gomorrah has long been held to be homosexuality as our English word "sodomy" indicates.
2. God warned earlier in Genesis 13:12-13, "Abram lived in the land of Canaan, while Lot lived among the cities of the plain and pitched his tents near Sodom. Now the men of Sodom were wicked and were sinning greatly against the LORD."
3. Genesis 18:20-21 reports, "Then the LORD said, 'The outcry against Sodom and Gomorrah is so great and their sin so grievous that I will go down and see if what they have done is as bad as the outcry that has reached me. If not, I will know.'"
4. Genesis 19:5 says, "They [the men of Sodom] called to Lot, 'Where are the men who came to you tonight? Bring them out to us so that we can have sex with them.'" This Hebrew word for sex is consistently translated as "sex" (e.g., 4:1, 4:17, 4:25, 24:16). Furthermore, the same word is used in Genesis 19:8 in saying that Lot's daughters had not had "sex" with any men.
5. The parallel account of Genesis 19 in Judges 19 likewise speaks of homosexual gang rape, which is likewise condemned there also.
6. Jude 7 says, "In a similar way, Sodom and Gomorrah and the surrounding towns gave themselves up to sexual immorality and perversion. They serve as an example of those who suffer the punishment of eternal fire."

There has long been a debate that the destruction of Sodom and Gomorrah is historical fiction. However, the archaeological evidence points to God destroying both towns and the surrounding areas for sexual sin. In the non-Christian Scientific Reports, it was first reported that archaeology Professor James Kennett, from the University of California at Santa Barbara, had found evidence of the destruction from the same time as the biblical account, in the same region, with the same devastation.[30,31]

Here is what was reported, "The biblical 'sin cities' of Sodom and Gomorrah could have been destroyed by a meteor 'cloudburst' that incinerated all 8,000 inhabitants... The giant space rock exploded over the town...creating a fireball...Now there seems to be hard evidence that a 'heavenly event' really did happen around that time. The cosmic calamity laid waste to the Jordan River Valley's northern shore, razing a huge 100-acre city to the ground. It also exterminated other cities and multiple small villages. There would have been no survivors...Detonation occurred about 2.5 miles above the ground. Even at that distance, the blast created a 740 mph shock wave...Human remains suggested they had been blown up or incinerated, with extreme disarticulation and fragmentation of bones. 'We saw evidence for temperatures greater than 2,000 degrees Celsius,' says study lead author Professor James Kennett of the University of California at Santa Barbara...An international team also found building materials and pottery shards melted into glass. Mud bricks had heat bubbles. These are all indications of unusually high temperatures, which would have occurred during the biblical account of the destruction of Sodom and Gomorrah. There was no man-made technology at the time that could have produced such astonishing damage...'There is evidence of a large cosmic fireball, close to Tall el-Hammam,' says Prof. Kennett. He likens the extraordinary event to the 1908 Tunguska Event when a 12 megaton meteor destroyed 80 million trees across 830 square miles of eastern Siberia..."[32]

Jude closes his stern warning against living in opposition to God by referring to a story from outside the Bible about people who acted like Satan, justified their rejection of God and godly authority, blasphemed the messengers of God, and were referred to as "unreasoning animals" who cannot be persuaded with wisdom or truth but are simply hell bent on destruction. Their root issues are, like Satan, independence and pride. Independent of God and godly authority and so proud as to rely on their own imagination that permit them to "defile the flesh" with sexual sin, they think they are superior to even the archangel Michael. He and Gabriel are the only two named holy angels in the Bible, and even Michael honored Satan, while demonic deceivers won't even honor the Lord.

Dig Deeper.
1. Read Genesis 18-19 to learn more about Sodom and Gomorrah.
2. Read Romans 1:18-32 to learn more about what Jude means by the phrases "sexual immorality" and "unnatural desire".
3. Read the following verses to learn more about Hell as a "punishment of eternal fire" – Daniel 12:2; Isaiah 66:18-24; Matthew 13:40-42; 2 Thessalonians 1:3-12; Revelation 20:14-15.

Walk it out. Talk it out.
1. Who are the evil examples that Jude uses to warn people of the coming judgment for sin? Which of these is most sobering to you? Why?
2. What are the evil behaviors, which will result in eternal punishment from Jesus Christ, that Jude uses to warn people?
3. What in Jude's warning is most haunting and concerning as you look at the state of the world, local

churches, and most importantly, yourself?
4. Is there anything on Jude's list that God has saved you from or you currently struggle with?
5. Is there anyone or anything we can be praying for?

<u>NOTES</u>

BLACK & WHITE IN A RAINBOW WORLD

Week 4: What Does God Think of Progressive Christianity?

Scripture to Read: Jude 11-16

Scripture for Memorization and Meditation:
Jude 14-15 – "Behold, the Lord comes with ten thousands of his holy ones, to execute judgment on all and to convict all the ungodly of all their deeds..."

Commentary:
    If you think of God's Word as having lines that should not be crossed, then you can think of progressivism in every generation as seeking to move that line. In the name of progress, thanks to increased learning to move us beyond the more primitive thinking of generations prior, every generation lives under the evolutionary myth that we are good and getting better, and that changing moral lines is how we make moral progress. In our day of global communication that is instant, the pace at which lines are moved is faster than ever. The eventual goal is always the same – to keep moving the line or standard of morality until there is no line. For example, since I was born, same sex attraction has gone from being a diagnosed mental health condition to a civil right complete with same sex marriage and a gender spectrum that denies God made us male and female. The next lines to be erased will be polygamy and the age of consent so that minors will be having sex with adults now that they have been sexualized by public school curriculum, entertainment, and social media platforms.
    The same battle we are fighting to hold the lines that God drew in His Word are not new. In Jude's day, he was writing to a church under attack from cultural forces in the world that were the same as in our day. One Bible commentary says, "The epistle of Jude is an impassioned exhortation to

a church that is being compromised. The writer's concerns, while touching on doctrine, are foremost ethical in nature. Posing a threat to the Christian community is a self-indulgent group that spurns spiritual authority and arrogantly appropriates its own authority."[33] To warn God's people in that day, and our day, Jude uses negative examples. This tactic is important – to help people become mature disciples, we need to tell them what God is for and what God is against. Why? Otherwise, they do both what God is for and against, which in God's eyes is like being in a covenant with Him and committing adultery on Him.

Jude's first negative example is Cain from Genesis 4. Like false believers in the church, Cain was supposed to love like a brother but ended up being a murderer.
The brothers Cain and Abel worked as a farmer and herdsmen, which are both honorable trades. As acts of worship, the brothers both brought offerings to the Lord, but the Lord rejected Cain's offering and received Abel's. This greatly angered Cain and the Lord warned Cain to control his anger lest it consume him and lead him into sin, the very thing that happened and resulted in a murder between the only two brothers on the earth. Jude's warning is that sometimes "brothers" in the church are murders like Cain.[a]

Jude's second negative example is "Balaam's error".[a] God became angry with Balaam because he was willing to be a false prophet and proclaim lies because he got paid well. In every age, false prophets are motived by false profits. The underlying sin is greed from lovers of money.

Jude's third negative example is "Korah's rebellion".[b] Korah rebelled against Moses, with no regard for his spiritual authority given from God. Jude is warning that some people in the church were just like Korah, defiant of God and godly leadership. The underlying sins are pride and independence,

---

[a] Numbers 22-24 [b] Numbers 16

which lead to rebellion and an insurrection. This is the same course of action as Satan and demons who led the first rebellion after which Korah modeled his rebellion.

One Bible commentator says, "When Jude sat down to compose his letter, he wanted to write about salvation, but felt compelled to caution his audience about false teachers who had slipped into their congregation (v. 3–4). His descriptions paint a scathing portrait of these spiritual charlatans. Stealthy and crafty, they presented themselves as bearers of the good news. Defensive walls wouldn't have helped the community Jude addressed, because these leaders were already inside."[34]

What makes these wolves so dangerous is that they were in the pen with the sheep and pretending to be sheep. Jesus warned of this very people in Matthew 7:15 saying, "Beware of false prophets, who come to you in sheep's clothing but inwardly are ravenous wolves." Jude says that these wolves had become friends with naïve and vulnerable people in the church, even having meals together in their homes like safe spiritual family members. Jesus goes on to say in Matthew 7:16-20, "You will recognize them by their fruits. Are grapes gathered from thornbushes, or figs from thistles? So, every healthy tree bears good fruit, but the diseased tree bears bad fruit. A healthy tree cannot bear bad fruit, nor can a diseased tree bear good fruit. Every tree that does not bear good fruit is cut down and thrown into the fire. Thus you will recognize them by their fruits."

Jude may have this teaching from his Big Brother Jesus in mind when he says that false believers are like clouds that do not rain, trees that do not bloom, seas that puke up lifeless foam, and stars that guide followers to nowhere. These people in Jude's day and our own make promises they do not keep and never achieve the kind of results they vow to accomplish. For example, in recent years, some false prophets said that if major American cities had less laws and less law enforcement officers, peace and prosperity would result. We now know that the exact opposite occurred, and cities looked a lot more like the burning of Hell than blessing of Heaven.

Like a crooked lying politician who has no intention of making good on any campaign promises, "These are grumblers, malcontents, following their own sinful desires; they are loud-mouthed boasters, showing favoritism to gain advantage." Jude warns us not to follow liars who want to lead us astray, promising that Jesus is returning with an angelic army to declare war on and utterly eviscerate this enemy of invaders saying, "the Lord comes with ten thousands of his holy ones, to execute judgment on all and to convict all the ungodly of all their deeds of ungodliness that they have committed in such an ungodly way, and of all the harsh things that ungodly sinners have spoken against him".

One Bible commentary says, "The Epistle of Jude warns of the dangers of false teachers, whose end is destruction. We are to be alert for them, to strengthen ourselves against spiritual deception, and to be ready to help vulnerable believers."[35]

Jude is encouraging believers to have the long view of things. For some people, this life is as close to Heaven as they will ever get, and eternal Hell awaits them. For other people, this life is as close to Hell as they will ever get, and eternal Heaven awaits them. Forever is a long time, and short-sided thinking leads to long-term suffering. The Christian is reminded that we must go through a little bit of hell on our way to Heaven, but Jesus is coming and when the time is right, all will be made right.

Dig Deeper.
1. To learn more about "Cain" read Genesis 4; Hebrews 11:4; 1 John 3:12-13.
2. To learn more about "Balaam's error" read Numbers

22-24.
3. To learn more about "Korah's rebellion" read Numbers 16.

Walk it out. Talk it out.
1. What are some of the most popular and powerful lies that people are believing in the world and Church today?
2. Read through Jude as a group and share aloud the negative things that Jude has to say about people who are false believers in the church using people and abusing the grace of God. Why is Jude so emphatically clear about this group of people?
3. What are some of the reasons that Christians will wrongly put up with people who are evil, harmful, and divisive? Has anyone in the group seen what happens to a church when these people are tolerated in the church for too long?
4. Since none of us has perfect theology or behavior, what are some beliefs or practices you've been vulnerable to and had to repent of since becoming a Christian?

NOTES

BLACK & WHITE IN A RAINBOW WORLD

A STUDY IN JUDE

Week 5: How to Stand Firm in a Woke World

Scripture to Read: Jude 17-25

Scripture for Memorization and Meditation:
Jude 24-25 – Now to him who is able to keep you from stumbling and to present you blameless before the presence of his glory with great joy, to the only God, our Savior, through Jesus Christ our Lord, be glory, majesty, dominion, and authority, before all time and now and forever. Amen.

Commentary:

The tone and tenor of Jude's letter makes sense to believers in our wayward and woke world. It feels like the demonic and evil world system has overtaken every aspect of the culture – politics, entertainment, education, business, and even the church. Some Bible commentators declare that Jude is the most negative book in the New Testament, and possibly the entire Bible.

Jude, however, is not negative. Jude is brutally and accurately honest. Up until this point in his letter, it reads a lot like Solomon's summary of our broken world in Ecclesiastes, looking only "under the sun". If we look out into the world, it is all darkness, discouragement and dread. The only hope for this world will not come from this world. We are all part of the problem, and so we cannot be the solution. We have made everything wrong and so we will not be able to make it right.

One Bible commentary says, "The brief Book of Jude was written by a man who wanted to write a positive treatise on salvation, but found himself driven to pen the New Testament's strongest condemnation of false teachers and teachings… His denunciation is blunt and powerful. And, in this day of ours when many seem willing to surrender truth in exchange for the sake of harmony, Jude's words may be especially important for us to heed."[36]

In our day, it is common for people to hate God so that they can love people. The truth is, to truly be loving means we must agree with and obey our God, who is the source and definition of love. What God says and does is loving, and any deviation from His commands and example is actually hating God, not loving Him. Furthermore, the most loving thing we can do for people who are sinners living apart from Jesus Christ is to tell them first the bad news of the gospel – that they are sinners who are wrong in the beliefs and behaviors – and then the good news – that Jesus alone is without sin and came to rescue and save sinners in love. To invite people to repentance of sin is loving, because it brings them to Jesus whose love will save them. To invite people to tolerance of sin is unloving, because it keeps them far from the love of Jesus and damns them.

For example, Illusionist and atheist Penn Jillette tells a story about getting handed a Bible after a show. "I wanted you to have this," the man said. "I'm kind of proselytizing. I'm a businessman. I'm sane. I'm not crazy." The man likely knew he was talking to a resolute atheist, but he was neither aggressive nor defensive. He just looked Jillette in the eye, said some kind words about the show, and gave his gift. The outspoken Jillette says this about the encounter: "I don't respect people who don't proselytize. I don't respect that at all. If you believe that there's a heaven and hell, and people could be going to hell—or not getting eternal life or whatever—and you think that, well, it's not really worth telling them this because it would make it socially awkward…How much do you have to hate somebody not to proselytize? How much do you have to hate somebody to believe that everlasting life is possible and not tell them that?"

Jillette concludes, "This guy was a really good guy. Polite and honest and sane—and he cared enough about me to proselytize and give me a Bible."[37]

There are always people who confuse being nice with being helpful. A good doctor is not as worried about saying nice things as with being honest and helpful so you can understand your problem and seek your solution. There are always people who want to take the gospel, which is offensive, and try to find a way to make it inoffensive, which is impossible. When people profess to be Christian leaders and teachers but are not saying what God says in His Word, they are leading believers astray and damaging the cause of evangelism, which seeks to introduce lost people to Jesus Christ.

Because the Bible is timeless, it never gets old but rather is always timely. Speaking to the prophetic and timeless book of Jude, Protestant Reformer John Calvin said roughly 500 years ago, "As unprincipled men, under the name of Christians, had crept in, whose chief object was to lead the unstable and weak to a profane contempt of God, Jude first shews, that the faithful ought not to have been moved by agents of this kind, by which the Church has always been assailed; and yet he exhorts them carefully to beware of such pests. And to render them more hateful and detestable, he denounces on them the approaching vengeance of God, such as their impiety deserved. Now, if we consider what Satan has attempted in our age, from the commencement of the revived gospel, and what arts he still busily employs to subvert the faith, and the fear of God, what was a useful warning in the time of Jude, is more than necessary in our age..."[38]

Today, things are certainly not better (arguably much worse). If Jude was vitally needed 500 years ago, the passage of time has only increased the degree of its timeliness.

Jude reminds us that we are living in the "last time" or last days. The Bible does not view history around years as much as around Jesus Christ. There were the days leading up to the life, death, burial, and resurrection of Jesus. Then, there was Jesus' earthly ministry and return to Heaven. Ever since, we are living in the "last time", which is the indefinite period of time between Jesus' first coming to save His people, and His Second Coming to raise the dead, sentence everyone to Heaven and Hell, finally destroy the demonic, lift the curse, and bless God's people in a perfect Kingdom together forever. The "last time" is the time between the day that Jesus went back in to Heaven and next time that He comes back to earth.

In this time between the times, believers are called to persevere. We are not to give up or give in. It has been promised that there will be "scoffers" who make fun of us, mock us, cancel us, fire us, mark our grades down in college and write us up for not playing by their rules in the workforce. The "scoffers" will be chasing "ungodly passions", causing "divisions, as "worldly people, devoid of the Spirit". Because they do not have the Spirit, they either live by the flesh, which is foolish, or the demonic, which is evil. They have no choice and we who have the Spirit are God's "beloved". We are commanded to not give up, but rather grow up, "building yourselves up in your most holy faith and praying in the Holy Spirit, keep yourselves in the love of God, waiting for the mercy of our Lord Jesus Christ that leads to eternal life".

One Bible commentator says, "Significant theological ideas in the Book of Jude are defense of the truths of the gospel; the necessity of moral purity and humility; and the perseverance of true believers, in spite of pernicious influences."[39]

The "building up" that Jude mentions would today be called Traditional Theory. The attackers who are deconstructing Christian belief and behavior today would be called Critical Theory. In another book I wrote called *Christian Theology vs Critical Theory*, which you can get for free in digital format in the store at RealFaith.com, I explain this at length. Unlike building something, which is hard, breaking something is easy.

Traditional theory is basically how we build things. Christianity would fit in with the concept of traditional theory. How do you build law and order? Our God is a God of law. His Word is filled with laws. How do you build a family? Scripture talks about husbands and wives, and it has specific things to say to both as it assumes God-assigned roles for our biological sex, gender identity, and sexuality. What's the best environment for raising a child? God made marriage and He made us male and female to marry, and then increase in number to fill the Earth, subdue it, and parent, raising our children in the admonition and instruction of the Lord according to Scripture. Simply stated, the Bible is a Traditional Theory. It is about how to build things like families, societies, theologies, economies, and legacies.

Critical Theory is basically how we break things that other people have built. It is a sledgehammer in the form of an overarching ideology or worldview that comes to dismantle pretty much anything that was previously built in a culture. Traditional Theory is about construction. Critical Theory is about demolition, also called deconstruction.

God works through Traditional Theory. Our God is Creator, Sustainer, and Redeemer who is about building perfectly and then faithfully rebuilding what sin has broken. Satan works through Critical Theory. Satan comes to steal what others have created, kill life in the Spirit, and brutally destroy whatever and whomever God loves.

When Jesus said, "I will build my church", Satan thought, "I will break that church." That is precisely what Jude is all about.

The reason we have not been taken home to Heaven, or seen Jesus' return, is because we have a mission to accomplish. Our mission, Jude says, is three-fold.

One, for those Christians who are struggling with doubt,

we need to put a lot of mercy on them and patiently and lovingly walk with them. Sometimes, these people have been through so much pain and hurt in their life that they are limping to Heaven slowly. Other times, these people have addictions that are deeply rooted, years of bad habits to overcome, trauma to heal from, or a long list of complicated questions about God they wrestle to answer.

Two, we are to act like firefighters and, by God's grace through God's Spirit by the power of the gospel of Jesus Christ, "save others by snatching them out of the fire". Sometimes, you need to buy your friend a Bible, tell them to start reading it, and check in that they are. Sometimes, you need to keep inviting that coworker to church and praying for their salvation. Sometimes, you need to research the questions and objections to Christianity that a family member has so that you can give them a thorough and detailed set of reasons for why you believe what you believe. Sometimes, you just need to lay hands over a hard-hearted person and ask the Holy Spirit to do what only He can do and change their heart. God saves people, and He sends us to be on this rescue mission with Him. God does not need us, but He invites us so that we can share in the joy of seeing Jesus save people and snatch them from the fire. There is nothing better than seeing people meet Jesus!

Three, we are instructed to keep "hating even the garment stained by the flesh". In Zechariah 3, there is a picture of Jesus trading clothes with us. He wears our dirty, filthy, rotten garments of sin on the cross, and we wear his spotless robes of righteousness through faith in Him. In the New Testament, we are repeatedly told to put off our old dirty way of life and put on our new clean way of life in the same way that we change our clothes.^a What Jude is saying is that if we love Jesus, we must hate the sin that killed our Savior. Once He

---

^a Rom. 13:12; 1 Cor. 15:53-54; Gal. 3:27; Eph. 4:24; Col. 3:9-10

has taken off our unrighteousness and worn it along with the wrath of God on the cross, we should seek to live in holiness, wearing His righteousness and not putting on the filthy and dirty sinful ways we wore before we met Jude's brother as our Savior.

Getting above the darkness of the world, Jude closes by pointing to the glory of God. This is one of the most awe-inspiring, heart-healing, mind-melting, and prayer-motivating declarations in the entire Bible. It is Jude's intention to get us to not just look out to our dark world but look up to our God who is the light of the world, hope of the world, Lord over the world, Savior in the world, and one day returning to judge the world. As you read it, notice the promise of "great joy". The emerging field of brain science tells us that throughout life, we are driven by either fear bonds or joy bonds. When we look out to the world, there is fear. When we look up to the lord in faith, there is joy. The key to overcoming fear bonds is to focus on the Lord, sing to the Lord, pray to the Lord, trust in the Lord, witness for the Lord, and build joy bonds in the Spirit so that we get above the clouds over us to the Lord over them.

Jude 24-25 – Now to him who is able to keep you from stumbling and to present you blameless before the presence of his glory with great joy, to the only God, our Savior, through Jesus Christ our Lord, be glory, majesty, dominion, and authority, before all time and now and forever. Amen.

Dig Deeper.
1. Jude says that some people are "devoid of the Spirit". Look up Romans 8:1-11 and Galatians 5:13-26 to learn more about what this looks like practically.
2. Look up the following Scriptures to learn more about putting on your new life in Christ – Zechariah 3; Romans 13:12; 1 Corinthians 15:53-54; Galatians

3:27; Ephesians 4:24; Colossians 3:9-10.

Walk it out. Talk it out.
1. What has been the big takeaway for you personally in studying Jude?
2. How has Jude helped you to interpret what is going in the culture of the world around you with beliefs and behaviors that are contrary to Christ but very popular and promoted?
3. What did you most struggle to accept in the book of Jude? Why?
4. Is there anyone or anything that the group can be praying for?
5. Why is it important to keep hope while we wait for Jesus' return? What does that look like practically?

NOTES

BLACK & WHITE IN A RAINBOW WORLD

A STUDY IN JUDE

ENDNOTES

1. Lawrence O. Richards, New International Encyclopedia of Bible Words: Based on the NIV and the NASB, Zondervan's Understand the Bible Reference Series (Grand Rapids, MI: Zondervan Publishing House, 1999), 226.

2. J. T. Dennison Jr., "Discern; Discerning; Discernment," ed. Geoffrey W. Bromiley, The International Standard Bible Encyclopedia, Revised (Wm. B. Eerdmans, 1979–1988), 947.

3. Charles Simeon, Horae Homileticae: James to Jude, vol. 20 (London: Holdsworth and Ball, 1833), 566.

4. Michael R. Jones, "Apostasy," ed. Douglas Mangum et al., Lexham Theological Wordbook, Lexham Bible Reference Series (Bellingham, WA: Lexham Press, 2014).

5. Grant R. Osborne, "Jude," in Cornerstone Biblical Commentary: James, 1–2 Peter, Jude, Revelation, ed. Philip W. Comfort, Cornerstone Biblical Commentary (Carol Stream, IL: Tyndale House Publishers, 2011), 359.

6. Erland Waltner and J. Daryl Charles, 1-2 Peter, Jude, Believers Church Bible Commentary (Scottdale, PA: Herald Press, 1999), 282.

7. Simon J. Kistemaker and William Hendriksen, Exposition of the Epistles of Peter and the Epistle of Jude, vol. 16, New Testament Commentary (Grand Rapids: Baker Book House, 1953–2001), 365.

8. D. J. Rowston, "The Most Neglected Book in the New Testament," NTS 21 (1974–75): 554–63.

9. William Barclay, ed., The Letters of John and Jude, Daily Study Bible Series (Philadelphia, PA: The Westminster John Knox Press, 1976), 157.

10. Ibid.

11. Matthew Henry, Matthew Henry's Commentary on the Whole Bible: Complete and Unabridged in One Volume (Peabody: Hendrickson, 1994), 2459.

12. Edward C. Pentecost, "Jude," in The Bible Knowledge Commentary: An Exposition of the Scriptures, ed. J. F. Walvoord and R. B. Zuck, vol. 2 (Wheaton, IL: Victor Books, 1985), 918.

13. Peter H. Davids, The Letters of 2 Peter and Jude, The Pillar New Testament Commentary (Grand Rapids, MI: William B. Eerdmans Pub. Co., 2006), 25.

14. (Origen, Comm. in Ev. Sec. Matt. 17.30 [Migne, PG, 13.1571]). Quoted in Erland Waltner and J. Daryl Charles, 1-2 Peter, Jude, Believers Church Bible Commentary (Scottdale, PA: Herald Press, 1999), 276.

15. Charles Meeks, "Christian," ed. John D. Barry et al., The Lexham Bible Dictionary (Bellingham, WA: Lexham Press, 2016).

16. "Who Was Jesus?" Larry King Live. First broadcast December 24, 2004, CNN, http://transcripts.cnn.com/TRANSCRIPTS/ 0412/24/lkl.01.html.

17. Dalai Lama, "The Karma of the Gospel," Newsweek, March 27, 2000.

18. Mahatma Gandhi, Harijan (March 6, 1937): 25.

19. H.E. Ecclesiastical History (Eusebius) II xxiii. 12–19). Quoted in D. A. Carson, The Gospel according to John, The Pillar New Testament Commentary (Leicester, England; Grand Rapids, MI: Inter-Varsity Press; W.B. Eerdmans, 1991), 389.

20. http://biblehub.com/library/pamphilius/church_history/chapter_xxiii_the_martyrdom_of_james.htm#1

21. James D. Tabor, "Testing a Hypothesis," Near Eastern Archaeology 69, no. 1–4 (2006): 133.

22. Michael Green, 2 Peter and Jude: An Introduction and

Commentary, vol. 18, Tyndale New Testament Commentaries (Downers Grove, IL: InterVarsity Press, 1987), 180.

23. Abraham, Ps. 105:42; Moses, Ne. 9:14; Rev. 15:3; David, Ps. 89:3; Daniel, Dn. 6:20.

24. R. C. Lucas and Christopher Green, The Message of 2 Peter & Jude: The Promise of His Coming, The Bible Speaks Today (Leicester, England; Downers Grove, IL: InterVarsity Press, 1995), 167.

25. William Arndt et al., A Greek-English Lexicon of the New Testament and Other Early Christian Literature (Chicago: University of Chicago Press, 2000), 356.

26. D. Edmond Hiebert, "Selected Studies from Jude Part 1: An Exposition of Jude 3–4," Bibliotheca Sacra 142 (1985): 144.

27. G. F. C. Fronmüller, "The Epistle General of Jude," in Lange's Commentary on the Holy Scriptures, with additions by J. Isidor Mombert (Grand Rapids: Zondervan Publishing House, n.d.), p. 13.

28. D. Edmond Hiebert, "Selected Studies from Jude Part 1: An Exposition of Jude 3–4," Bibliotheca Sacra 142 (1985): 144.

29. Warren W. Wiersbe, The Bible Exposition Commentary, vol. 2 (Wheaton, IL: Victor Books, 1996), 548.

30. https://www.nature.com/articles/s41598-021-97778-3/figures/1

31. https://www.news.ucsb.edu/2021/020400/ancient-disaster

32. https://www.nature.com/articles/s41598-021-97778-3

33. Erland Waltner and J. Daryl Charles, 1-2 Peter, Jude, Believers Church Bible Commentary (Scottdale, PA: Herald Press, 1999), 274.

34. John D. Barry and Miles Custis, 2 Peter & Jude: Contend for the Faith, Not Your Average Bible Study (Bellingham, WA: Lexham Press, 2014), 5.

35. David Walls and Max Anders, I & II Peter, I, II & III John, Jude, vol. 11, Holman New Testament Commentary (Nashville, TN: Broadman & Holman Publishers, 1999), 260.

36. Lawrence O. Richards, The Bible Reader's Companion, electronic ed. (Wheaton: Victor Books, 1991), 899.

37. https://www.youtube.com/watch?time_continue=2&v=owZc3Xq8obk

38. John Calvin, Jude, electronic ed., Calvin's Commentaries (Albany, OR: Ages Software, 1998).

39. William H. Baker, "Jude," in Evangelical Commentary on the Bible, vol. 3, Baker Reference Library (Grand Rapids, MI: Baker Book House, 1995), 1191.

ABOUT MARK DRISCOLL & REALFAITH

With Pastor Mark, it's all about Jesus! He is a spiritual leader, prolific author, and compelling speaker, but at his core, he is a family man. Mark and his wife Grace have been married and doing vocational ministry together since 1993 and, along with their five kids, planted Trinity Church in Scottsdale, Arizona as a family ministry.

Pastor Mark, Grace, and their oldest daughter, Ashley, also started RealFaith Ministries, which contains a mountain of Bible teaching for men, women, couples, parents, pastors, leaders, Spanish speakers, and more, which you can access by visiting **RealFaith.com** or downloading the **RealFaith app**.

With a master's degree in exegetical theology from Western Seminary in Portland, Oregon, he has spent the better part of his life teaching verse-by-verse through books of the Bible, contextualizing its timeless truths and never shying away from challenging, convicting passages that speak to the heart of current cultural dilemmas.

Together, Mark and Grace have co-authored *Win Your War*, *Real Marriage*, and *Real Romance: Sex in the Song of Songs* and he co-authored a father-daughter project called *Pray Like*

Jesus with his daughter, Ashley. Pastor Mark has also written numerous other books including *Spirit-Filled Jesus*, *Who Do You Think You Are?*, *Vintage Jesus*, and *Doctrine*.

If you have any prayer requests for us, questions for future Ask Pastor Mark or Dear Grace videos, or a testimony regarding how God has used this and other resources to help you learn God's Word, we would love to hear from you at **hello@realfaith.com**.

DATE _____

HUNTING PLACE _____

☐ LAKE ☐ MARSH ☐ JUMP SHOOTING ☐ POTHOLES ☐ SHORELAND ☐ FIELD HUNT

NEAREST CITY _____

DIRECTION FROM CITY: ☐ N ☐ S ☐ E ☐ W MILES _____

ARRIVAL TIME _____ DEPARTURE TIME _____

HUNTING COMPANIONS: _____
_____
_____

WEATHER: ☐ SUNNY ☐ PARTLY CLOUDY ☐ LIGHT OVERCAST ☐ HEAVY OVERCAST

☐ RAIN ☐ DRIZZLE ☐ MIST ☐ FOG ☐ SLEET ☐ SNOW

TEMPERATURE: ☐ WARM ☐ COOL ☐ COLD _____ DEGREES

WIND DIRECTION, A.M. _____, P.M. _____ VELOCITY _____ ☐ NO WIND

☐ DECOY SHOOTING NUMBER OF DECOYS USED: _____ DUCKS _____ GEESE

☐ PASS SHOOTING CROP RESIDUE (FIELD HUNT) _____

☐ DUCK CALL ☐ GOOSE CALL COMMENTS: _____

NOTES: _____
_____
_____
_____
_____
_____
_____
_____

Continued on Next Page

DATE_____

SPECIES BAGGED	NUMBER		COMMENTS
	DRAKES	HENS	
MALLARD			
PINTAIL			
WIDGEON			
GADWALL			
BLUEWING TEAL			
GREENWING TEAL			
SHOVELER			
BLACK DUCK			
WOOD DUCK			
CANVASBACK			
REDHEAD			
BLUEBILL			
RINGBILL			
RUDDY & OTHER			
CANADA GEESE	Greater	Lesser	
WHITE FRONTED GEESE	Adult	Juvenile	
SNOW GEESE			
BLUE GEESE			

☐ BIRD LEG BAND RECOVERED ON SPECIES:_____

NO. ON BAND: _____

☐ REPORTED TO U.S. F&WS ON DATE _____

RESPONSE: BIRD BAND DATE_____ BANDED WHERE?_____

DATE _____

HUNTING PLACE _____

☐ LAKE   ☐ MARSH   ☐ JUMP SHOOTING ☐ POTHOLES ☐ SHORELAND   ☐ FIELD HUNT

NEAREST CITY _____

DIRECTION FROM CITY: ☐ N   ☐ S   ☐ E   ☐ W   MILES _____

ARRIVAL TIME _____ DEPARTURE TIME _____

HUNTING COMPANIONS: _____
_____
_____

WEATHER: ☐ SUNNY   ☐ PARTLY CLOUDY   ☐ LIGHT OVERCAST   ☐ HEAVY OVERCAST
           ☐ RAIN   ☐ DRIZZLE   ☐ MIST   ☐ FOG   ☐ SLEET   ☐ SNOW

TEMPERATURE: ☐ WARM   ☐ COOL   ☐ COLD   _____ DEGREES

WIND DIRECTION, A.M. _____, P.M. _____ VELOCITY _____ ☐ NO WIND

☐ DECOY SHOOTING   NUMBER OF DECOYS USED: _____ DUCKS _____ GEESE

☐ PASS SHOOTING   CROP RESIDUE (FIELD HUNT) _____

☐ DUCK CALL   ☐ GOOSE CALL   COMMENTS: _____

NOTES: _____
_____
_____
_____
_____
_____
_____
_____
_____

DATE_____

SPECIES BAGGED	NUMBER		COMMENTS
	DRAKES	HENS	
MALLARD			
PINTAIL			
WIDGEON			
GADWALL			
BLUEWING TEAL			
GREENWING TEAL			
SHOVELER			
BLACK DUCK			
WOOD DUCK			
CANVASBACK			
REDHEAD			
BLUEBILL			
RINGBILL			
RUDDY & OTHER			
CANADA GEESE	Greater	Lesser	
WHITE FRONTED GEESE	Adult	Juvenile	
SNOW GEESE			
BLUE GEESE			

☐ BIRD LEG BAND RECOVERED ON SPECIES:_____

NO. ON BAND: _____

☐ REPORTED TO U.S. F&WS ON DATE _____

RESPONSE: BIRD BAND DATE_____ BANDED WHERE?_____

DATE _____

HUNTING PLACE _____

☐ LAKE   ☐ MARSH   ☐ JUMP SHOOTING ☐ POTHOLES ☐ SHORELAND   ☐ FIELD HUNT

NEAREST CITY _____

DIRECTION FROM CITY: ☐ N   ☐ S   ☐ E   ☐ W   MILES _____

ARRIVAL TIME _____ DEPARTURE TIME _____

HUNTING COMPANIONS: _____
_____
_____

WEATHER: ☐ SUNNY   ☐ PARTLY CLOUDY   ☐ LIGHT OVERCAST   ☐ HEAVY OVERCAST
           ☐ RAIN   ☐ DRIZZLE   ☐ MIST   ☐ FOG   ☐ SLEET   ☐ SNOW

TEMPERATURE: ☐ WARM   ☐ COOL   ☐ COLD   _____ DEGREES

WIND DIRECTION, A.M. _____, P.M. _____ VELOCITY _____   ☐ NO WIND

☐ DECOY SHOOTING   NUMBER OF DECOYS USED: _____ DUCKS _____ GEESE

☐ PASS SHOOTING   CROP RESIDUE (FIELD HUNT) _____

☐ DUCK CALL   ☐ GOOSE CALL   COMMENTS: _____

NOTES: _____
_____
_____
_____
_____
_____
_____
_____
_____

Continued on Next Page

DATE_____

SPECIES BAGGED	NUMBER		COMMENTS
	DRAKES	HENS	
MALLARD			
PINTAIL			
WIDGEON			
GADWALL			
BLUEWING TEAL			
GREENWING TEAL			
SHOVELER			
BLACK DUCK			
WOOD DUCK			
CANVASBACK			
REDHEAD			
BLUEBILL			
RINGBILL			
RUDDY & OTHER			
CANADA GEESE	Greater	Lesser	
WHITE FRONTED GEESE	Adult	Juvenile	
SNOW GEESE			
BLUE GEESE			

☐ BIRD LEG BAND RECOVERED ON SPECIES:_____

NO. ON BAND: _____

☐ REPORTED TO U.S. F&WS ON DATE _____

RESPONSE: BIRD BAND DATE_____ BANDED WHERE?_____

DATE _____

HUNTING PLACE _____

☐ LAKE   ☐ MARSH   ☐ JUMP SHOOTING ☐ POTHOLES ☐ SHORELAND   ☐ FIELD HUNT

NEAREST CITY _____

DIRECTION FROM CITY: ☐ N   ☐ S   ☐ E   ☐ W   MILES _____

ARRIVAL TIME _____ DEPARTURE TIME _____

HUNTING COMPANIONS: _____
_____
_____

WEATHER: ☐ SUNNY   ☐ PARTLY CLOUDY   ☐ LIGHT OVERCAST   ☐ HEAVY OVERCAST
            ☐ RAIN   ☐ DRIZZLE   ☐ MIST   ☐ FOG   ☐ SLEET   ☐ SNOW

TEMPERATURE: ☐ WARM   ☐ COOL   ☐ COLD   _____ DEGREES

WIND DIRECTION, A.M. _____, P.M. _____   VELOCITY _____   ☐ NO WIND

☐ DECOY SHOOTING   NUMBER OF DECOYS USED: _____ DUCKS _____ GEESE

☐ PASS SHOOTING   CROP RESIDUE (FIELD HUNT) _____

☐ DUCK CALL   ☐ GOOSE CALL   COMMENTS: _____

NOTES: _____
_____
_____
_____
_____
_____
_____
_____
_____

Continued on Next Page

DATE_____

SPECIES BAGGED	NUMBER		COMMENTS
	DRAKES	HENS	
MALLARD			
PINTAIL			
WIDGEON			
GADWALL			
BLUEWING TEAL			
GREENWING TEAL			
SHOVELER			
BLACK DUCK			
WOOD DUCK			
CANVASBACK			
REDHEAD			
BLUEBILL			
RINGBILL			
RUDDY & OTHER			
CANADA GEESE	Greater	Lesser	
WHITE FRONTED GEESE	Adult	Juvenile	
SNOW GEESE			
BLUE GEESE			

☐ BIRD LEG BAND RECOVERED ON SPECIES:_____

NO. ON BAND: _____

☐ REPORTED TO U.S. F&WS ON DATE _____

RESPONSE: BIRD BAND DATE_____ BANDED WHERE?_____

DATE _____

HUNTING PLACE _____

☐ LAKE   ☐ MARSH   ☐ JUMP SHOOTING ☐ POTHOLES ☐ SHORELAND   ☐ FIELD HUNT

NEAREST CITY _____

DIRECTION FROM CITY: ☐ N   ☐ S   ☐ E   ☐ W   MILES _____

ARRIVAL TIME _____ DEPARTURE TIME _____

HUNTING COMPANIONS: _____

_____

_____

WEATHER: ☐ SUNNY   ☐ PARTLY CLOUDY   ☐ LIGHT OVERCAST   ☐ HEAVY OVERCAST

           ☐ RAIN   ☐ DRIZZLE   ☐ MIST   ☐ FOG   ☐ SLEET   ☐ SNOW

TEMPERATURE: ☐ WARM   ☐ COOL   ☐ COLD   _____ DEGREES

WIND DIRECTION, A.M. _____, P.M. _____ VELOCITY _____ ☐ NO WIND

☐ DECOY SHOOTING   NUMBER OF DECOYS USED: _____ DUCKS _____ GEESE

☐ PASS SHOOTING   CROP RESIDUE (FIELD HUNT) _____

☐ DUCK CALL   ☐ GOOSE CALL   COMMENTS: _____

NOTES: _____

_____

_____

_____

_____

_____

_____

_____

_____

Continued on Next Page

DATE_____

SPECIES BAGGED	NUMBER		COMMENTS
	DRAKES	HENS	
MALLARD			
PINTAIL			
WIDGEON			
GADWALL			
BLUEWING TEAL			
GREENWING TEAL			
SHOVELER			
BLACK DUCK			
WOOD DUCK			
CANVASBACK			
REDHEAD			
BLUEBILL			
RINGBILL			
RUDDY & OTHER			
CANADA GEESE	Greater	Lesser	
WHITE FRONTED GEESE	Adult	Juvenile	
SNOW GEESE			
BLUE GEESE			

☐ BIRD LEG BAND RECOVERED ON SPECIES:_____

NO. ON BAND: _____

☐ REPORTED TO U.S. F&WS ON DATE _____

RESPONSE: BIRD BAND DATE_____ BANDED WHERE?_____

DATE _____

HUNTING PLACE _____

☐ LAKE   ☐ MARSH   ☐ JUMP SHOOTING ☐ POTHOLES ☐ SHORELAND   ☐ FIELD HUNT

NEAREST CITY _____

DIRECTION FROM CITY: ☐ N   ☐ S   ☐ E   ☐ W   MILES _____

ARRIVAL TIME _____ DEPARTURE TIME _____

HUNTING COMPANIONS: _____
_____
_____

WEATHER: ☐ SUNNY   ☐ PARTLY CLOUDY   ☐ LIGHT OVERCAST   ☐ HEAVY OVERCAST
           ☐ RAIN   ☐ DRIZZLE   ☐ MIST   ☐ FOG   ☐ SLEET   ☐ SNOW

TEMPERATURE: ☐ WARM   ☐ COOL   ☐ COLD   _____ DEGREES

WIND DIRECTION, A.M. _____, P.M. _____ VELOCITY _____ ☐ NO WIND

☐ DECOY SHOOTING   NUMBER OF DECOYS USED: _____ DUCKS _____ GEESE

☐ PASS SHOOTING   CROP RESIDUE (FIELD HUNT) _____

☐ DUCK CALL   ☐ GOOSE CALL   COMMENTS: _____

NOTES: _____
_____
_____
_____
_____
_____
_____
_____
_____

Continued on Next Page

DATE_____

SPECIES BAGGED	NUMBER		COMMENTS
	DRAKES	HENS	
MALLARD			
PINTAIL			
WIDGEON			
GADWALL			
BLUEWING TEAL			
GREENWING TEAL			
SHOVELER			
BLACK DUCK			
WOOD DUCK			
CANVASBACK			
REDHEAD			
BLUEBILL			
RINGBILL			
RUDDY & OTHER			
CANADA GEESE	Greater	Lesser	
WHITE FRONTED GEESE	Adult	Juvenile	
SNOW GEESE			
BLUE GEESE			

☐ BIRD LEG BAND RECOVERED ON SPECIES:_____

NO. ON BAND: _____

☐ REPORTED TO U.S. F&WS ON DATE _____

RESPONSE: BIRD BAND DATE_____ BANDED WHERE?_____

DATE _____

HUNTING PLACE _____

☐ LAKE ☐ MARSH ☐ JUMP SHOOTING ☐ POTHOLES ☐ SHORELAND ☐ FIELD HUNT

NEAREST CITY _____

DIRECTION FROM CITY: ☐ N   ☐ S   ☐ E   ☐ W   MILES _____

ARRIVAL TIME _____ DEPARTURE TIME _____

HUNTING COMPANIONS: _____
_____
_____

WEATHER: ☐ SUNNY   ☐ PARTLY CLOUDY   ☐ LIGHT OVERCAST   ☐ HEAVY OVERCAST
          ☐ RAIN   ☐ DRIZZLE   ☐ MIST   ☐ FOG   ☐ SLEET   ☐ SNOW

TEMPERATURE: ☐ WARM   ☐ COOL   ☐ COLD   _____ DEGREES

WIND DIRECTION, A.M. _____, P.M. _____ VELOCITY _____ ☐ NO WIND

☐ DECOY SHOOTING   NUMBER OF DECOYS USED: _____ DUCKS _____ GEESE

☐ PASS SHOOTING   CROP RESIDUE (FIELD HUNT) _____

☐ DUCK CALL   ☐ GOOSE CALL   COMMENTS: _____

_____

NOTES: _____
_____
_____
_____
_____
_____
_____
_____
_____

Continued on Next Page

DATE_____

SPECIES BAGGED	NUMBER		COMMENTS
	DRAKES	HENS	
MALLARD			
PINTAIL			
WIDGEON			
GADWALL			
BLUEWING TEAL			
GREENWING TEAL			
SHOVELER			
BLACK DUCK			
WOOD DUCK			
CANVASBACK			
REDHEAD			
BLUEBILL			
RINGBILL			
RUDDY & OTHER			
CANADA GEESE	Greater	Lesser	
WHITE FRONTED GEESE	Adult	Juvenile	
SNOW GEESE			
BLUE GEESE			

☐ BIRD LEG BAND RECOVERED ON SPECIES:_____

NO. ON BAND: _____

☐ REPORTED TO U.S. F&WS ON DATE _____

RESPONSE: BIRD BAND DATE_____ BANDED WHERE?_____

DATE _____

HUNTING PLACE _____

☐ LAKE   ☐ MARSH   ☐ JUMP SHOOTING ☐ POTHOLES ☐ SHORELAND   ☐ FIELD HUNT

NEAREST CITY _____

DIRECTION FROM CITY: ☐ N   ☐ S   ☐ E   ☐ W   MILES _____

ARRIVAL TIME _____ DEPARTURE TIME _____

HUNTING COMPANIONS: _____

_____

_____

WEATHER: ☐ SUNNY   ☐ PARTLY CLOUDY   ☐ LIGHT OVERCAST   ☐ HEAVY OVERCAST

           ☐ RAIN   ☐ DRIZZLE   ☐ MIST   ☐ FOG   ☐ SLEET   ☐ SNOW

TEMPERATURE: ☐ WARM   ☐ COOL   ☐ COLD   _____ DEGREES

WIND DIRECTION, A.M. _____, P.M. _____ VELOCITY _____   ☐ NO WIND

☐ DECOY SHOOTING   NUMBER OF DECOYS USED: _____ DUCKS _____ GEESE

☐ PASS SHOOTING   CROP RESIDUE (FIELD HUNT) _____

☐ DUCK CALL   ☐ GOOSE CALL   COMMENTS: _____

NOTES: _____

_____

_____

_____

_____

_____

_____

_____

Continued on Next Page

DATE_____

SPECIES BAGGED	NUMBER		COMMENTS
	DRAKES	HENS	
MALLARD			
PINTAIL			
WIDGEON			
GADWALL			
BLUEWING TEAL			
GREENWING TEAL			
SHOVELER			
BLACK DUCK			
WOOD DUCK			
CANVASBACK			
REDHEAD			
BLUEBILL			
RINGBILL			
RUDDY & OTHER			
CANADA GEESE	Greater	Lesser	
WHITE FRONTED GEESE	Adult	Juvenile	
SNOW GEESE			
BLUE GEESE			

☐ BIRD LEG BAND RECOVERED ON SPECIES:_____

NO. ON BAND: _____

☐ REPORTED TO U.S. F&WS ON DATE _____

RESPONSE: BIRD BAND DATE_____ BANDED WHERE?_____

DATE _____

HUNTING PLACE _____

☐ LAKE   ☐ MARSH   ☐ JUMP SHOOTING   ☐ POTHOLES   ☐ SHORELAND   ☐ FIELD HUNT

NEAREST CITY _____

DIRECTION FROM CITY: ☐ N   ☐ S   ☐ E   ☐ W   MILES _____

ARRIVAL TIME _____ DEPARTURE TIME _____

HUNTING COMPANIONS: _____
_____
_____

WEATHER: ☐ SUNNY   ☐ PARTLY CLOUDY   ☐ LIGHT OVERCAST   ☐ HEAVY OVERCAST
           ☐ RAIN   ☐ DRIZZLE   ☐ MIST   ☐ FOG   ☐ SLEET   ☐ SNOW

TEMPERATURE: ☐ WARM   ☐ COOL   ☐ COLD   _____ DEGREES

WIND DIRECTION, A.M. _____, P.M. _____ VELOCITY _____   ☐ NO WIND

☐ DECOY SHOOTING   NUMBER OF DECOYS USED: _____ DUCKS _____ GEESE

☐ PASS SHOOTING   CROP RESIDUE (FIELD HUNT) _____

☐ DUCK CALL   ☐ GOOSE CALL   COMMENTS: _____

NOTES: _____
_____
_____
_____
_____
_____
_____
_____
_____

Continued on Next Page

DATE _____

SPECIES BAGGED	NUMBER		COMMENTS
	DRAKES	HENS	
MALLARD			
PINTAIL			
WIDGEON			
GADWALL			
BLUEWING TEAL			
GREENWING TEAL			
SHOVELER			
BLACK DUCK			
WOOD DUCK			
CANVASBACK			
REDHEAD			
BLUEBILL			
RINGBILL			
RUDDY & OTHER			
CANADA GEESE	Greater	Lesser	
WHITE FRONTED GEESE	Adult	Juvenile	
SNOW GEESE			
BLUE GEESE			

☐ BIRD LEG BAND RECOVERED ON SPECIES: _____

NO. ON BAND: _____

☐ REPORTED TO U.S. F&WS ON DATE _____

RESPONSE: BIRD BAND DATE _____ BANDED WHERE? _____

DATE _____

HUNTING PLACE _____

☐ LAKE ☐ MARSH ☐ JUMP SHOOTING ☐ POTHOLES ☐ SHORELAND ☐ FIELD HUNT

NEAREST CITY _____

DIRECTION FROM CITY: ☐ N   ☐ S   ☐ E   ☐ W   MILES _____

ARRIVAL TIME _____ DEPARTURE TIME _____

HUNTING COMPANIONS: _____
_____
_____

WEATHER: ☐ SUNNY   ☐ PARTLY CLOUDY   ☐ LIGHT OVERCAST   ☐ HEAVY OVERCAST
          ☐ RAIN   ☐ DRIZZLE   ☐ MIST   ☐ FOG   ☐ SLEET   ☐ SNOW

TEMPERATURE: ☐ WARM   ☐ COOL   ☐ COLD   _____ DEGREES

WIND DIRECTION, A.M. _____, P.M. _____ VELOCITY _____ ☐ NO WIND

☐ DECOY SHOOTING   NUMBER OF DECOYS USED: _____ DUCKS _____ GEESE

☐ PASS SHOOTING   CROP RESIDUE (FIELD HUNT) _____

☐ DUCK CALL   ☐ GOOSE CALL   COMMENTS: _____

NOTES: _____
_____
_____
_____
_____
_____
_____
_____
_____

Continued on Next Page

DATE_____

SPECIES BAGGED	NUMBER		COMMENTS
	DRAKES	HENS	
MALLARD			
PINTAIL			
WIDGEON			
GADWALL			
BLUEWING TEAL			
GREENWING TEAL			
SHOVELER			
BLACK DUCK			
WOOD DUCK			
CANVASBACK			
REDHEAD			
BLUEBILL			
RINGBILL			
RUDDY & OTHER			
CANADA GEESE	Greater	Lesser	
WHITE FRONTED GEESE	Adult	Juvenile	
SNOW GEESE			
BLUE GEESE			

☐ BIRD LEG BAND RECOVERED ON SPECIES:_____

NO. ON BAND: _____

☐ REPORTED TO U.S. F&WS ON DATE _____

RESPONSE: BIRD BAND DATE_____ BANDED WHERE?_____

DATE _____

HUNTING PLACE _____

☐ LAKE   ☐ MARSH   ☐ JUMP SHOOTING ☐ POTHOLES ☐ SHORELAND   ☐ FIELD HUNT

NEAREST CITY _____

DIRECTION FROM CITY: ☐ N   ☐ S   ☐ E   ☐ W   MILES _____

ARRIVAL TIME _____ DEPARTURE TIME _____

HUNTING COMPANIONS: _____

_____

_____

WEATHER: ☐ SUNNY   ☐ PARTLY CLOUDY   ☐ LIGHT OVERCAST   ☐ HEAVY OVERCAST

☐ RAIN   ☐ DRIZZLE   ☐ MIST   ☐ FOG   ☐ SLEET   ☐ SNOW

TEMPERATURE: ☐ WARM   ☐ COOL   ☐ COLD   _____ DEGREES

WIND DIRECTION, A.M. _____, P.M. _____ VELOCITY _____   ☐ NO WIND

☐ DECOY SHOOTING   NUMBER OF DECOYS USED: _____ DUCKS _____ GEESE

☐ PASS SHOOTING   CROP RESIDUE (FIELD HUNT) _____

☐ DUCK CALL   ☐ GOOSE CALL   COMMENTS: _____

NOTES: _____

_____

_____

_____

_____

_____

_____

_____

Continued on Next Page

DATE _____

SPECIES BAGGED	NUMBER		COMMENTS
	DRAKES	HENS	
MALLARD			
PINTAIL			
WIDGEON			
GADWALL			
BLUEWING TEAL			
GREENWING TEAL			
SHOVELER			
BLACK DUCK			
WOOD DUCK			
CANVASBACK			
REDHEAD			
BLUEBILL			
RINGBILL			
RUDDY & OTHER			
CANADA GEESE	Greater	Lesser	
WHITE FRONTED GEESE	Adult	Juvenile	
SNOW GEESE			
BLUE GEESE			

☐ BIRD LEG BAND RECOVERED ON SPECIES: _____

NO. ON BAND: _____

☐ REPORTED TO U.S. F&WS ON DATE _____

RESPONSE: BIRD BAND DATE _____ BANDED WHERE? _____

DATE _____

HUNTING PLACE _____

☐ LAKE   ☐ MARSH   ☐ JUMP SHOOTING ☐ POTHOLES ☐ SHORELAND   ☐ FIELD HUNT

NEAREST CITY _____

DIRECTION FROM CITY: ☐ N   ☐ S   ☐ E   ☐ W   MILES _____

ARRIVAL TIME _____ DEPARTURE TIME _____

HUNTING COMPANIONS: _____
_____
_____

WEATHER: ☐ SUNNY   ☐ PARTLY CLOUDY   ☐ LIGHT OVERCAST   ☐ HEAVY OVERCAST
           ☐ RAIN   ☐ DRIZZLE   ☐ MIST   ☐ FOG   ☐ SLEET   ☐ SNOW

TEMPERATURE: ☐ WARM   ☐ COOL   ☐ COLD   _____DEGREES

WIND DIRECTION, A.M._____, P.M._____ VELOCITY_____ ☐ NO WIND

☐ DECOY SHOOTING   NUMBER OF DECOYS USED:_____DUCKS _____GEESE

☐ PASS SHOOTING   CROP RESIDUE (FIELD HUNT) _____

☐ DUCK CALL   ☐ GOOSE CALL   COMMENTS: _____

NOTES: _____
_____
_____
_____
_____
_____
_____
_____
_____

Continued on Next Page

DATE_____

SPECIES BAGGED	NUMBER		COMMENTS
	DRAKES	HENS	
MALLARD			
PINTAIL			
WIDGEON			
GADWALL			
BLUEWING TEAL			
GREENWING TEAL			
SHOVELER			
BLACK DUCK			
WOOD DUCK			
CANVASBACK			
REDHEAD			
BLUEBILL			
RINGBILL			
RUDDY & OTHER			
CANADA GEESE	Greater	Lesser	
WHITE FRONTED GEESE	Adult	Juvenile	
SNOW GEESE			
BLUE GEESE			

☐ BIRD LEG BAND RECOVERED ON SPECIES:_____

NO. ON BAND: _____

☐ REPORTED TO U.S. F&WS ON DATE _____

RESPONSE: BIRD BAND DATE_____ BANDED WHERE?_____

DATE _____

HUNTING PLACE _____

☐ LAKE   ☐ MARSH   ☐ JUMP SHOOTING ☐ POTHOLES ☐ SHORELAND   ☐ FIELD HUNT

NEAREST CITY _____

DIRECTION FROM CITY: ☐ N   ☐ S   ☐ E   ☐ W   MILES _____

ARRIVAL TIME _____ DEPARTURE TIME _____

HUNTING COMPANIONS: _____
_____
_____

WEATHER: ☐ SUNNY   ☐ PARTLY CLOUDY   ☐ LIGHT OVERCAST   ☐ HEAVY OVERCAST
           ☐ RAIN   ☐ DRIZZLE   ☐ MIST   ☐ FOG   ☐ SLEET   ☐ SNOW

TEMPERATURE: ☐ WARM   ☐ COOL   ☐ COLD   _____ DEGREES

WIND DIRECTION, A.M. _____, P.M. _____ VELOCITY _____   ☐ NO WIND

☐ DECOY SHOOTING   NUMBER OF DECOYS USED: _____ DUCKS _____ GEESE

☐ PASS SHOOTING   CROP RESIDUE (FIELD HUNT) _____

☐ DUCK CALL   ☐ GOOSE CALL   COMMENTS: _____

NOTES: _____
_____
_____
_____
_____
_____
_____
_____
_____

Continued on Next Page

DATE_____

SPECIES BAGGED	NUMBER		COMMENTS
	DRAKES	HENS	
MALLARD			
PINTAIL			
WIDGEON			
GADWALL			
BLUEWING TEAL			
GREENWING TEAL			
SHOVELER			
BLACK DUCK			
WOOD DUCK			
CANVASBACK			
REDHEAD			
BLUEBILL			
RINGBILL			
RUDDY & OTHER			
CANADA GEESE	Greater	Lesser	
WHITE FRONTED GEESE	Adult	Juvenile	
SNOW GEESE			
BLUE GEESE			

☐ BIRD LEG BAND RECOVERED ON SPECIES:_____

NO. ON BAND: _____

☐ REPORTED TO U.S. F&WS ON DATE _____

RESPONSE: BIRD BAND DATE_____ BANDED WHERE?_____

DATE _____

HUNTING PLACE _____

☐ LAKE   ☐ MARSH   ☐ JUMP SHOOTING ☐ POTHOLES ☐ SHORELAND   ☐ FIELD HUNT

NEAREST CITY _____

DIRECTION FROM CITY: ☐ N   ☐ S   ☐ E   ☐ W   MILES _____

ARRIVAL TIME _____ DEPARTURE TIME _____

HUNTING COMPANIONS: _____
_____
_____

WEATHER: ☐ SUNNY   ☐ PARTLY CLOUDY   ☐ LIGHT OVERCAST   ☐ HEAVY OVERCAST
           ☐ RAIN   ☐ DRIZZLE   ☐ MIST   ☐ FOG   ☐ SLEET   ☐ SNOW

TEMPERATURE: ☐ WARM   ☐ COOL   ☐ COLD   _____ DEGREES

WIND DIRECTION, A.M. _____, P.M. _____ VELOCITY _____ ☐ NO WIND

☐ DECOY SHOOTING   NUMBER OF DECOYS USED: _____ DUCKS _____ GEESE

☐ PASS SHOOTING   CROP RESIDUE (FIELD HUNT) _____

☐ DUCK CALL   ☐ GOOSE CALL   COMMENTS: _____

NOTES: _____
_____
_____
_____
_____
_____
_____
_____
_____

Continued on Next Page

DATE _____

SPECIES BAGGED	NUMBER		COMMENTS
	DRAKES	HENS	
MALLARD			
PINTAIL			
WIDGEON			
GADWALL			
BLUEWING TEAL			
GREENWING TEAL			
SHOVELER			
BLACK DUCK			
WOOD DUCK			
CANVASBACK			
REDHEAD			
BLUEBILL			
RINGBILL			
RUDDY & OTHER			
CANADA GEESE	Greater	Lesser	
WHITE FRONTED GEESE	Adult	Juvenile	
SNOW GEESE			
BLUE GEESE			

☐ BIRD LEG BAND RECOVERED ON SPECIES: _____

NO. ON BAND: _____

☐ REPORTED TO U.S. F&WS ON DATE _____

RESPONSE: BIRD BAND DATE _____ BANDED WHERE? _____

DATE _____

HUNTING PLACE _____

☐ LAKE ☐ MARSH ☐ JUMP SHOOTING ☐ POTHOLES ☐ SHORELAND ☐ FIELD HUNT

NEAREST CITY _____

DIRECTION FROM CITY: ☐ N   ☐ S   ☐ E   ☐ W   MILES _____

ARRIVAL TIME _____ DEPARTURE TIME _____

HUNTING COMPANIONS: _____
_____
_____

WEATHER: ☐ SUNNY   ☐ PARTLY CLOUDY   ☐ LIGHT OVERCAST   ☐ HEAVY OVERCAST
          ☐ RAIN   ☐ DRIZZLE   ☐ MIST   ☐ FOG   ☐ SLEET   ☐ SNOW

TEMPERATURE: ☐ WARM   ☐ COOL   ☐ COLD   _____ DEGREES

WIND DIRECTION, A.M. _____, P.M. _____ VELOCITY _____ ☐ NO WIND

☐ DECOY SHOOTING   NUMBER OF DECOYS USED: _____ DUCKS _____ GEESE

☐ PASS SHOOTING   CROP RESIDUE (FIELD HUNT) _____

☐ DUCK CALL   ☐ GOOSE CALL   COMMENTS: _____

NOTES: _____
_____
_____
_____
_____
_____
_____
_____
_____

Continued on Next Page

DATE_____

SPECIES BAGGED	NUMBER		COMMENTS
	DRAKES	HENS	
MALLARD			
PINTAIL			
WIDGEON			
GADWALL			
BLUEWING TEAL			
GREENWING TEAL			
SHOVELER			
BLACK DUCK			
WOOD DUCK			
CANVASBACK			
REDHEAD			
BLUEBILL			
RINGBILL			
RUDDY & OTHER			
CANADA GEESE	Greater	Lesser	
WHITE FRONTED GEESE	Adult	Juvenile	
SNOW GEESE			
BLUE GEESE			

☐ BIRD LEG BAND RECOVERED ON SPECIES:_____

NO. ON BAND: _____

☐ REPORTED TO U.S. F&WS ON DATE _____

RESPONSE: BIRD BAND DATE_____ BANDED WHERE?_____

DATE _____

HUNTING PLACE _____

☐ LAKE   ☐ MARSH   ☐ JUMP SHOOTING ☐ POTHOLES ☐ SHORELAND   ☐ FIELD HUNT

NEAREST CITY _____

DIRECTION FROM CITY: ☐ N   ☐ S   ☐ E   ☐ W   MILES _____

ARRIVAL TIME _____ DEPARTURE TIME _____

HUNTING COMPANIONS: _____
_____
_____

WEATHER: ☐ SUNNY   ☐ PARTLY CLOUDY   ☐ LIGHT OVERCAST   ☐ HEAVY OVERCAST
           ☐ RAIN   ☐ DRIZZLE   ☐ MIST   ☐ FOG   ☐ SLEET   ☐ SNOW

TEMPERATURE: ☐ WARM   ☐ COOL   ☐ COLD   _____ DEGREES

WIND DIRECTION, A.M. _____, P.M. _____ VELOCITY _____   ☐ NO WIND

☐ DECOY SHOOTING   NUMBER OF DECOYS USED: _____ DUCKS _____ GEESE

☐ PASS SHOOTING   CROP RESIDUE (FIELD HUNT) _____

☐ DUCK CALL   ☐ GOOSE CALL   COMMENTS: _____

NOTES: _____
_____
_____
_____
_____
_____
_____
_____
_____

Continued on Next Page

DATE_____

SPECIES BAGGED	NUMBER		COMMENTS
	DRAKES	HENS	
MALLARD			
PINTAIL			
WIDGEON			
GADWALL			
BLUEWING TEAL			
GREENWING TEAL			
SHOVELER			
BLACK DUCK			
WOOD DUCK			
CANVASBACK			
REDHEAD			
BLUEBILL			
RINGBILL			
RUDDY & OTHER			
CANADA GEESE	Greater	Lesser	
WHITE FRONTED GEESE	Adult	Juvenile	
SNOW GEESE			
BLUE GEESE			

☐ BIRD LEG BAND RECOVERED ON SPECIES:_____

NO. ON BAND: _____

☐ REPORTED TO U.S. F&WS ON DATE _____

RESPONSE: BIRD BAND DATE_____ BANDED WHERE?_____

DATE _____

HUNTING PLACE _____

☐ LAKE ☐ MARSH ☐ JUMP SHOOTING ☐ POTHOLES ☐ SHORELAND ☐ FIELD HUNT

NEAREST CITY _____

DIRECTION FROM CITY: ☐ N   ☐ S   ☐ E   ☐ W   MILES _____

ARRIVAL TIME _____ DEPARTURE TIME _____

HUNTING COMPANIONS: _____
_____
_____

WEATHER: ☐ SUNNY   ☐ PARTLY CLOUDY   ☐ LIGHT OVERCAST   ☐ HEAVY OVERCAST
           ☐ RAIN   ☐ DRIZZLE   ☐ MIST   ☐ FOG   ☐ SLEET   ☐ SNOW

TEMPERATURE: ☐ WARM   ☐ COOL   ☐ COLD   _____ DEGREES

WIND DIRECTION, A.M. _____, P.M. _____ VELOCITY _____ ☐ NO WIND

☐ DECOY SHOOTING   NUMBER OF DECOYS USED: _____ DUCKS _____ GEESE

☐ PASS SHOOTING   CROP RESIDUE (FIELD HUNT) _____

☐ DUCK CALL   ☐ GOOSE CALL   COMMENTS: _____

NOTES: _____
_____
_____
_____
_____
_____
_____
_____
_____

Continued on Next Page

DATE_____

SPECIES BAGGED	NUMBER		COMMENTS
	DRAKES	HENS	
MALLARD			
PINTAIL			
WIDGEON			
GADWALL			
BLUEWING TEAL			
GREENWING TEAL			
SHOVELER			
BLACK DUCK			
WOOD DUCK			
CANVASBACK			
REDHEAD			
BLUEBILL			
RINGBILL			
RUDDY & OTHER			
CANADA GEESE	Greater	Lesser	
WHITE FRONTED GEESE	Adult	Juvenile	
SNOW GEESE			
BLUE GEESE			

☐ BIRD LEG BAND RECOVERED ON SPECIES:_____

NO. ON BAND: _____

☐ REPORTED TO U.S. F&WS ON DATE _____

RESPONSE: BIRD BAND DATE_____ BANDED WHERE?_____

DATE _____

HUNTING PLACE _____

☐ LAKE ☐ MARSH ☐ JUMP SHOOTING ☐ POTHOLES ☐ SHORELAND ☐ FIELD HUNT

NEAREST CITY _____

DIRECTION FROM CITY: ☐ N   ☐ S   ☐ E   ☐ W   MILES _____

ARRIVAL TIME _____ DEPARTURE TIME _____

HUNTING COMPANIONS: _____

_____

_____

WEATHER: ☐ SUNNY   ☐ PARTLY CLOUDY   ☐ LIGHT OVERCAST   ☐ HEAVY OVERCAST

          ☐ RAIN   ☐ DRIZZLE   ☐ MIST   ☐ FOG   ☐ SLEET   ☐ SNOW

TEMPERATURE: ☐ WARM   ☐ COOL   ☐ COLD   _____ DEGREES

WIND DIRECTION, A.M._____, P.M._____ VELOCITY_____ ☐ NO WIND

☐ DECOY SHOOTING   NUMBER OF DECOYS USED:_____ DUCKS _____ GEESE

☐ PASS SHOOTING   CROP RESIDUE (FIELD HUNT) _____

☐ DUCK CALL   ☐ GOOSE CALL   COMMENTS: _____

NOTES: _____

_____

_____

_____

_____

_____

_____

_____

_____

Continued on Next Page

DATE_____

SPECIES BAGGED	NUMBER		COMMENTS
	DRAKES	HENS	
MALLARD			
PINTAIL			
WIDGEON			
GADWALL			
BLUEWING TEAL			
GREENWING TEAL			
SHOVELER			
BLACK DUCK			
WOOD DUCK			
CANVASBACK			
REDHEAD			
BLUEBILL			
RINGBILL			
RUDDY & OTHER			
CANADA GEESE	Greater	Lesser	
WHITE FRONTED GEESE	Adult	Juvenile	
SNOW GEESE			
BLUE GEESE			

☐ BIRD LEG BAND RECOVERED ON SPECIES:_____

NO. ON BAND: _____

☐ REPORTED TO U.S. F&WS ON DATE _____

RESPONSE: BIRD BAND DATE_____ BANDED WHERE?_____

DATE _____

HUNTING PLACE _____

☐ LAKE ☐ MARSH ☐ JUMP SHOOTING ☐ POTHOLES ☐ SHORELAND ☐ FIELD HUNT

NEAREST CITY _____

DIRECTION FROM CITY: ☐ N   ☐ S   ☐ E   ☐ W   MILES _____

ARRIVAL TIME _____ DEPARTURE TIME _____

HUNTING COMPANIONS: _____

_____

_____

WEATHER: ☐ SUNNY   ☐ PARTLY CLOUDY   ☐ LIGHT OVERCAST   ☐ HEAVY OVERCAST

☐ RAIN ☐ DRIZZLE ☐ MIST ☐ FOG ☐ SLEET ☐ SNOW

TEMPERATURE: ☐ WARM   ☐ COOL   ☐ COLD   _____ DEGREES

WIND DIRECTION, A.M. _____, P.M. _____ VELOCITY _____ ☐ NO WIND

☐ DECOY SHOOTING   NUMBER OF DECOYS USED: _____ DUCKS _____ GEESE

☐ PASS SHOOTING   CROP RESIDUE (FIELD HUNT) _____

☐ DUCK CALL   ☐ GOOSE CALL   COMMENTS: _____

NOTES: _____

_____

_____

_____

_____

_____

_____

_____

_____

Continued on Next Page

DATE_____

SPECIES BAGGED	NUMBER		COMMENTS
	DRAKES	HENS	
MALLARD			
PINTAIL			
WIDGEON			
GADWALL			
BLUEWING TEAL			
GREENWING TEAL			
SHOVELER			
BLACK DUCK			
WOOD DUCK			
CANVASBACK			
REDHEAD			
BLUEBILL			
RINGBILL			
RUDDY & OTHER			
CANADA GEESE	Greater	Lesser	
WHITE FRONTED GEESE	Adult	Juvenile	
SNOW GEESE			
BLUE GEESE			

☐ BIRD LEG BAND RECOVERED ON SPECIES:_____

NO. ON BAND: _____

☐ REPORTED TO U.S. F&WS ON DATE _____

RESPONSE: BIRD BAND DATE_____ BANDED WHERE?_____

DATE _____

HUNTING PLACE _____

☐ LAKE ☐ MARSH ☐ JUMP SHOOTING ☐ POTHOLES ☐ SHORELAND ☐ FIELD HUNT

NEAREST CITY _____

DIRECTION FROM CITY: ☐ N ☐ S ☐ E ☐ W MILES _____

ARRIVAL TIME _____ DEPARTURE TIME _____

HUNTING COMPANIONS: _____

_____

_____

WEATHER: ☐ SUNNY ☐ PARTLY CLOUDY ☐ LIGHT OVERCAST ☐ HEAVY OVERCAST

☐ RAIN ☐ DRIZZLE ☐ MIST ☐ FOG ☐ SLEET ☐ SNOW

TEMPERATURE: ☐ WARM ☐ COOL ☐ COLD _____ DEGREES

WIND DIRECTION, A.M. _____, P.M. _____ VELOCITY _____ ☐ NO WIND

☐ DECOY SHOOTING NUMBER OF DECOYS USED: _____ DUCKS _____ GEESE

☐ PASS SHOOTING CROP RESIDUE (FIELD HUNT) _____

☐ DUCK CALL ☐ GOOSE CALL COMMENTS: _____

NOTES: _____

_____

_____

_____

_____

_____

_____

_____

_____

Continued on Next Page

DATE_____

SPECIES BAGGED	NUMBER		COMMENTS
	DRAKES	HENS	
MALLARD			
PINTAIL			
WIDGEON			
GADWALL			
BLUEWING TEAL			
GREENWING TEAL			
SHOVELER			
BLACK DUCK			
WOOD DUCK			
CANVASBACK			
REDHEAD			
BLUEBILL			
RINGBILL			
RUDDY & OTHER			
CANADA GEESE	Greater	Lesser	
WHITE FRONTED GEESE	Adult	Juvenile	
SNOW GEESE			
BLUE GEESE			

☐ BIRD LEG BAND RECOVERED ON SPECIES:_____

NO. ON BAND: _____

☐ REPORTED TO U.S. F&WS ON DATE _____

RESPONSE: BIRD BAND DATE_____ BANDED WHERE?_____

DATE _____

HUNTING PLACE _____

☐ LAKE ☐ MARSH ☐ JUMP SHOOTING ☐ POTHOLES ☐ SHORELAND ☐ FIELD HUNT

NEAREST CITY _____

DIRECTION FROM CITY: ☐ N   ☐ S   ☐ E   ☐ W   MILES _____

ARRIVAL TIME _____ DEPARTURE TIME _____

HUNTING COMPANIONS: _____
_____
_____

WEATHER: ☐ SUNNY   ☐ PARTLY CLOUDY   ☐ LIGHT OVERCAST   ☐ HEAVY OVERCAST
          ☐ RAIN   ☐ DRIZZLE   ☐ MIST   ☐ FOG   ☐ SLEET   ☐ SNOW

TEMPERATURE: ☐ WARM   ☐ COOL   ☐ COLD   _____ DEGREES

WIND DIRECTION, A.M. _____, P.M. _____ VELOCITY _____ ☐ NO WIND

☐ DECOY SHOOTING   NUMBER OF DECOYS USED: _____ DUCKS _____ GEESE

☐ PASS SHOOTING   CROP RESIDUE (FIELD HUNT) _____

☐ DUCK CALL   ☐ GOOSE CALL   COMMENTS: _____

NOTES: _____
_____
_____
_____
_____
_____
_____
_____
_____

Continued on Next Page

DATE_____

SPECIES BAGGED	NUMBER		COMMENTS
	DRAKES	HENS	
MALLARD			
PINTAIL			
WIDGEON			
GADWALL			
BLUEWING TEAL			
GREENWING TEAL			
SHOVELER			
BLACK DUCK			
WOOD DUCK			
CANVASBACK			
REDHEAD			
BLUEBILL			
RINGBILL			
RUDDY & OTHER			
CANADA GEESE	Greater	Lesser	
WHITE FRONTED GEESE	Adult	Juvenile	
SNOW GEESE			
BLUE GEESE			

☐ BIRD LEG BAND RECOVERED ON SPECIES:_____

NO. ON BAND: _____

☐ REPORTED TO U.S. F&WS ON DATE _____

RESPONSE: BIRD BAND DATE_____ BANDED WHERE?_____

DATE _____

HUNTING PLACE _____

☐ LAKE   ☐ MARSH   ☐ JUMP SHOOTING ☐ POTHOLES ☐ SHORELAND   ☐ FIELD HUNT

NEAREST CITY _____

DIRECTION FROM CITY: ☐ N   ☐ S   ☐ E   ☐ W   MILES _____

ARRIVAL TIME _____ DEPARTURE TIME _____

HUNTING COMPANIONS: _____
_____
_____

WEATHER: ☐ SUNNY   ☐ PARTLY CLOUDY   ☐ LIGHT OVERCAST   ☐ HEAVY OVERCAST
           ☐ RAIN   ☐ DRIZZLE   ☐ MIST   ☐ FOG   ☐ SLEET   ☐ SNOW

TEMPERATURE: ☐ WARM   ☐ COOL   ☐ COLD   _____ DEGREES

WIND DIRECTION, A.M._____, P.M._____ VELOCITY_____ ☐ NO WIND

☐ DECOY SHOOTING   NUMBER OF DECOYS USED:_____ DUCKS _____ GEESE

☐ PASS SHOOTING   CROP RESIDUE (FIELD HUNT) _____

☐ DUCK CALL   ☐ GOOSE CALL   COMMENTS: _____

NOTES: _____
_____
_____
_____
_____
_____
_____
_____
_____

Continued on Next Page

DATE_____

SPECIES BAGGED	NUMBER		COMMENTS
	DRAKES	HENS	
MALLARD			
PINTAIL			
WIDGEON			
GADWALL			
BLUEWING TEAL			
GREENWING TEAL			
SHOVELER			
BLACK DUCK			
WOOD DUCK			
CANVASBACK			
REDHEAD			
BLUEBILL			
RINGBILL			
RUDDY & OTHER			
CANADA GEESE	Greater	Lesser	
WHITE FRONTED GEESE	Adult	Juvenile	
SNOW GEESE			
BLUE GEESE			

☐ BIRD LEG BAND RECOVERED ON SPECIES:_____

NO. ON BAND: _____

☐ REPORTED TO U.S. F&WS ON DATE _____

RESPONSE: BIRD BAND DATE_____ BANDED WHERE?_____

DATE _____

HUNTING PLACE _____

☐ LAKE ☐ MARSH ☐ JUMP SHOOTING ☐ POTHOLES ☐ SHORELAND ☐ FIELD HUNT

NEAREST CITY _____

DIRECTION FROM CITY: ☐ N   ☐ S   ☐ E   ☐ W   MILES _____

ARRIVAL TIME _____ DEPARTURE TIME _____

HUNTING COMPANIONS: _____
_____
_____

WEATHER: ☐ SUNNY   ☐ PARTLY CLOUDY   ☐ LIGHT OVERCAST   ☐ HEAVY OVERCAST
          ☐ RAIN ☐ DRIZZLE ☐ MIST ☐ FOG ☐ SLEET ☐ SNOW

TEMPERATURE: ☐ WARM   ☐ COOL   ☐ COLD   _____ DEGREES

WIND DIRECTION, A.M. _____, P.M. _____ VELOCITY _____ ☐ NO WIND

☐ DECOY SHOOTING   NUMBER OF DECOYS USED: _____ DUCKS _____ GEESE

☐ PASS SHOOTING   CROP RESIDUE (FIELD HUNT) _____

☐ DUCK CALL   ☐ GOOSE CALL   COMMENTS: _____

NOTES: _____
_____
_____
_____
_____
_____
_____
_____
_____

Continued on Next Page

DATE_____

SPECIES BAGGED	NUMBER		COMMENTS
	DRAKES	HENS	
MALLARD			
PINTAIL			
WIDGEON			
GADWALL			
BLUEWING TEAL			
GREENWING TEAL			
SHOVELER			
BLACK DUCK			
WOOD DUCK			
CANVASBACK			
REDHEAD			
BLUEBILL			
RINGBILL			
RUDDY & OTHER			
CANADA GEESE	Greater	Lesser	
WHITE FRONTED GEESE	Adult	Juvenile	
SNOW GEESE			
BLUE GEESE			

☐ BIRD LEG BAND RECOVERED ON SPECIES:_____

NO. ON BAND: _____

☐ REPORTED TO U.S. F&WS ON DATE _____

RESPONSE: BIRD BAND DATE_____ BANDED WHERE?_____

DATE _____

HUNTING PLACE _____

☐ LAKE   ☐ MARSH   ☐ JUMP SHOOTING ☐ POTHOLES ☐ SHORELAND   ☐ FIELD HUNT

NEAREST CITY _____

DIRECTION FROM CITY: ☐ N   ☐ S   ☐ E   ☐ W   MILES _____

ARRIVAL TIME _____ DEPARTURE TIME _____

HUNTING COMPANIONS: _____
_____
_____

WEATHER: ☐ SUNNY   ☐ PARTLY CLOUDY   ☐ LIGHT OVERCAST   ☐ HEAVY OVERCAST
           ☐ RAIN   ☐ DRIZZLE   ☐ MIST   ☐ FOG   ☐ SLEET   ☐ SNOW

TEMPERATURE: ☐ WARM   ☐ COOL   ☐ COLD   _____DEGREES

WIND DIRECTION, A.M._____, P.M._____ VELOCITY_____ ☐ NO WIND

☐ DECOY SHOOTING   NUMBER OF DECOYS USED:_____DUCKS _____GEESE

☐ PASS SHOOTING   CROP RESIDUE (FIELD HUNT) _____

☐ DUCK CALL   ☐ GOOSE CALL   COMMENTS: _____

NOTES: _____
_____
_____
_____
_____
_____
_____
_____
_____

Continued on Next Page

DATE _____

SPECIES BAGGED	NUMBER		COMMENTS
	DRAKES	HENS	
MALLARD			
PINTAIL			
WIDGEON			
GADWALL			
BLUEWING TEAL			
GREENWING TEAL			
SHOVELER			
BLACK DUCK			
WOOD DUCK			
CANVASBACK			
REDHEAD			
BLUEBILL			
RINGBILL			
RUDDY & OTHER			
CANADA GEESE	Greater	Lesser	
WHITE FRONTED GEESE	Adult	Juvenile	
SNOW GEESE			
BLUE GEESE			

☐ BIRD LEG BAND RECOVERED ON SPECIES: _____

NO. ON BAND: _____

☐ REPORTED TO U.S. F&WS ON DATE _____

RESPONSE: BIRD BAND DATE _____ BANDED WHERE? _____

DATE _____

HUNTING PLACE _____

☐ LAKE ☐ MARSH ☐ JUMP SHOOTING ☐ POTHOLES ☐ SHORELAND ☐ FIELD HUNT

NEAREST CITY _____

DIRECTION FROM CITY: ☐ N   ☐ S   ☐ E   ☐ W   MILES _____

ARRIVAL TIME _____ DEPARTURE TIME _____

HUNTING COMPANIONS: _____
_____
_____

WEATHER: ☐ SUNNY   ☐ PARTLY CLOUDY   ☐ LIGHT OVERCAST   ☐ HEAVY OVERCAST
          ☐ RAIN   ☐ DRIZZLE   ☐ MIST   ☐ FOG   ☐ SLEET   ☐ SNOW

TEMPERATURE: ☐ WARM   ☐ COOL   ☐ COLD   _____ DEGREES

WIND DIRECTION, A.M. _____, P.M. _____ VELOCITY _____ ☐ NO WIND

☐ DECOY SHOOTING   NUMBER OF DECOYS USED: _____ DUCKS _____ GEESE

☐ PASS SHOOTING   CROP RESIDUE (FIELD HUNT) _____

☐ DUCK CALL   ☐ GOOSE CALL   COMMENTS: _____

NOTES: _____
_____
_____
_____
_____
_____
_____
_____
_____

Continued on Next Page

DATE _____

SPECIES BAGGED	NUMBER		COMMENTS
	DRAKES	HENS	
MALLARD			
PINTAIL			
WIDGEON			
GADWALL			
BLUEWING TEAL			
GREENWING TEAL			
SHOVELER			
BLACK DUCK			
WOOD DUCK			
CANVASBACK			
REDHEAD			
BLUEBILL			
RINGBILL			
RUDDY & OTHER			
CANADA GEESE	Greater	Lesser	
WHITE FRONTED GEESE	Adult	Juvenile	
SNOW GEESE			
BLUE GEESE			

☐ BIRD LEG BAND RECOVERED ON SPECIES:_____

NO. ON BAND: _____

☐ REPORTED TO U.S. F&WS ON DATE _____

RESPONSE: BIRD BAND DATE_____ BANDED WHERE?_____

DATE _____

HUNTING PLACE _____

☐ LAKE ☐ MARSH ☐ JUMP SHOOTING ☐ POTHOLES ☐ SHORELAND ☐ FIELD HUNT

NEAREST CITY _____

DIRECTION FROM CITY: ☐ N   ☐ S   ☐ E   ☐ W   MILES _____

ARRIVAL TIME _____ DEPARTURE TIME _____

HUNTING COMPANIONS: _____

_____

_____

WEATHER: ☐ SUNNY   ☐ PARTLY CLOUDY   ☐ LIGHT OVERCAST   ☐ HEAVY OVERCAST

☐ RAIN   ☐ DRIZZLE   ☐ MIST   ☐ FOG   ☐ SLEET   ☐ SNOW

TEMPERATURE: ☐ WARM   ☐ COOL   ☐ COLD   _____ DEGREES

WIND DIRECTION, A.M. _____, P.M. _____ VELOCITY _____ ☐ NO WIND

☐ DECOY SHOOTING   NUMBER OF DECOYS USED: _____ DUCKS _____ GEESE

☐ PASS SHOOTING   CROP RESIDUE (FIELD HUNT) _____

☐ DUCK CALL   ☐ GOOSE CALL   COMMENTS: _____

NOTES: _____

_____

_____

_____

_____

_____

_____

_____

_____

Continued on Next Page

DATE_____

SPECIES BAGGED	NUMBER		COMMENTS
	DRAKES	HENS	
MALLARD			
PINTAIL			
WIDGEON			
GADWALL			
BLUEWING TEAL			
GREENWING TEAL			
SHOVELER			
BLACK DUCK			
WOOD DUCK			
CANVASBACK			
REDHEAD			
BLUEBILL			
RINGBILL			
RUDDY & OTHER			
CANADA GEESE	Greater	Lesser	
WHITE FRONTED GEESE	Adult	Juvenile	
SNOW GEESE			
BLUE GEESE			

☐ BIRD LEG BAND RECOVERED ON SPECIES:_____

NO. ON BAND: _____

☐ REPORTED TO U.S. F&WS ON DATE _____

RESPONSE: BIRD BAND DATE_____ BANDED WHERE?_____

DATE _____

HUNTING PLACE _____

☐ LAKE ☐ MARSH ☐ JUMP SHOOTING ☐ POTHOLES ☐ SHORELAND ☐ FIELD HUNT

NEAREST CITY _____

DIRECTION FROM CITY: ☐ N ☐ S ☐ E ☐ W MILES _____

ARRIVAL TIME _____ DEPARTURE TIME _____

HUNTING COMPANIONS: _____
_____
_____

WEATHER: ☐ SUNNY ☐ PARTLY CLOUDY ☐ LIGHT OVERCAST ☐ HEAVY OVERCAST
          ☐ RAIN ☐ DRIZZLE ☐ MIST ☐ FOG ☐ SLEET ☐ SNOW

TEMPERATURE: ☐ WARM ☐ COOL ☐ COLD _____ DEGREES

WIND DIRECTION, A.M. _____, P.M. _____ VELOCITY _____ ☐ NO WIND

☐ DECOY SHOOTING NUMBER OF DECOYS USED: _____ DUCKS _____ GEESE

☐ PASS SHOOTING CROP RESIDUE (FIELD HUNT) _____

☐ DUCK CALL ☐ GOOSE CALL COMMENTS: _____

NOTES: _____
_____
_____
_____
_____
_____
_____
_____
_____

Continued on Next Page

DATE_____

SPECIES BAGGED	NUMBER		COMMENTS
	DRAKES	HENS	
MALLARD			
PINTAIL			
WIDGEON			
GADWALL			
BLUEWING TEAL			
GREENWING TEAL			
SHOVELER			
BLACK DUCK			
WOOD DUCK			
CANVASBACK			
REDHEAD			
BLUEBILL			
RINGBILL			
RUDDY & OTHER			
CANADA GEESE	Greater	Lesser	
WHITE FRONTED GEESE	Adult	Juvenile	
SNOW GEESE			
BLUE GEESE			

☐ BIRD LEG BAND RECOVERED ON SPECIES:_____

NO. ON BAND: _____

☐ REPORTED TO U.S. F&WS ON DATE _____

RESPONSE: BIRD BAND DATE_____ BANDED WHERE?_____

DATE _____

HUNTING PLACE _____

☐ LAKE   ☐ MARSH   ☐ JUMP SHOOTING   ☐ POTHOLES   ☐ SHORELAND   ☐ FIELD HUNT

NEAREST CITY _____

DIRECTION FROM CITY: ☐ N   ☐ S   ☐ E   ☐ W   MILES _____

ARRIVAL TIME _____ DEPARTURE TIME _____

HUNTING COMPANIONS: _____
_____
_____

WEATHER: ☐ SUNNY   ☐ PARTLY CLOUDY   ☐ LIGHT OVERCAST   ☐ HEAVY OVERCAST
           ☐ RAIN   ☐ DRIZZLE   ☐ MIST   ☐ FOG   ☐ SLEET   ☐ SNOW

TEMPERATURE: ☐ WARM   ☐ COOL   ☐ COLD   _____ DEGREES

WIND DIRECTION, A.M. _____, P.M. _____ VELOCITY _____   ☐ NO WIND

☐ DECOY SHOOTING   NUMBER OF DECOYS USED: _____ DUCKS _____ GEESE

☐ PASS SHOOTING   CROP RESIDUE (FIELD HUNT) _____

☐ DUCK CALL   ☐ GOOSE CALL   COMMENTS: _____

NOTES: _____
_____
_____
_____
_____
_____
_____
_____
_____

Continued on Next Page

DATE _____

SPECIES BAGGED	NUMBER		COMMENTS
	DRAKES	HENS	
MALLARD			
PINTAIL			
WIDGEON			
GADWALL			
BLUEWING TEAL			
GREENWING TEAL			
SHOVELER			
BLACK DUCK			
WOOD DUCK			
CANVASBACK			
REDHEAD			
BLUEBILL			
RINGBILL			
RUDDY & OTHER			
CANADA GEESE	Greater	Lesser	
WHITE FRONTED GEESE	Adult	Juvenile	
SNOW GEESE			
BLUE GEESE			

☐ BIRD LEG BAND RECOVERED ON SPECIES: _____

NO. ON BAND: _____

☐ REPORTED TO U.S. F&WS ON DATE _____

RESPONSE: BIRD BAND DATE _____ BANDED WHERE? _____

DATE _____

HUNTING PLACE _____

☐ LAKE   ☐ MARSH   ☐ JUMP SHOOTING ☐ POTHOLES ☐ SHORELAND   ☐ FIELD HUNT

NEAREST CITY _____

DIRECTION FROM CITY: ☐ N   ☐ S   ☐ E   ☐ W   MILES _____

ARRIVAL TIME _____ DEPARTURE TIME _____

HUNTING COMPANIONS: _____
_____
_____

WEATHER: ☐ SUNNY   ☐ PARTLY CLOUDY   ☐ LIGHT OVERCAST   ☐ HEAVY OVERCAST
           ☐ RAIN   ☐ DRIZZLE   ☐ MIST   ☐ FOG   ☐ SLEET   ☐ SNOW

TEMPERATURE: ☐ WARM   ☐ COOL   ☐ COLD   _____ DEGREES

WIND DIRECTION, A.M. _____, P.M. _____ VELOCITY _____ ☐ NO WIND

☐ DECOY SHOOTING   NUMBER OF DECOYS USED: _____ DUCKS _____ GEESE

☐ PASS SHOOTING   CROP RESIDUE (FIELD HUNT) _____

☐ DUCK CALL   ☐ GOOSE CALL   COMMENTS: _____

NOTES: _____
_____
_____
_____
_____
_____
_____
_____

Continued on Next Page

DATE_____

SPECIES BAGGED	NUMBER		COMMENTS
	DRAKES	HENS	
MALLARD			
PINTAIL			
WIDGEON			
GADWALL			
BLUEWING TEAL			
GREENWING TEAL			
SHOVELER			
BLACK DUCK			
WOOD DUCK			
CANVASBACK			
REDHEAD			
BLUEBILL			
RINGBILL			
RUDDY & OTHER			
CANADA GEESE	Greater	Lesser	
WHITE FRONTED GEESE	Adult	Juvenile	
SNOW GEESE			
BLUE GEESE			

☐ BIRD LEG BAND RECOVERED ON SPECIES:_____

NO. ON BAND: _____

☐ REPORTED TO U.S. F&WS ON DATE _____

RESPONSE: BIRD BAND DATE_____ BANDED WHERE?_____

DATE _____

HUNTING PLACE _____

☐ LAKE ☐ MARSH ☐ JUMP SHOOTING ☐ POTHOLES ☐ SHORELAND ☐ FIELD HUNT

NEAREST CITY _____

DIRECTION FROM CITY: ☐ N   ☐ S   ☐ E   ☐ W   MILES _____

ARRIVAL TIME _____ DEPARTURE TIME _____

HUNTING COMPANIONS: _____

_____

_____

WEATHER: ☐ SUNNY   ☐ PARTLY CLOUDY   ☐ LIGHT OVERCAST   ☐ HEAVY OVERCAST

          ☐ RAIN   ☐ DRIZZLE   ☐ MIST   ☐ FOG   ☐ SLEET   ☐ SNOW

TEMPERATURE: ☐ WARM   ☐ COOL   ☐ COLD   _____ DEGREES

WIND DIRECTION, A.M. _____, P.M. _____ VELOCITY _____ ☐ NO WIND

☐ DECOY SHOOTING   NUMBER OF DECOYS USED: _____ DUCKS _____ GEESE

☐ PASS SHOOTING   CROP RESIDUE (FIELD HUNT) _____

☐ DUCK CALL   ☐ GOOSE CALL   COMMENTS: _____

NOTES: _____

_____

_____

_____

_____

_____

_____

_____

_____

Continued on Next Page

DATE_____

SPECIES BAGGED	NUMBER		COMMENTS
	DRAKES	HENS	
MALLARD			
PINTAIL			
WIDGEON			
GADWALL			
BLUEWING TEAL			
GREENWING TEAL			
SHOVELER			
BLACK DUCK			
WOOD DUCK			
CANVASBACK			
REDHEAD			
BLUEBILL			
RINGBILL			
RUDDY & OTHER			
CANADA GEESE	Greater	Lesser	
WHITE FRONTED GEESE	Adult	Juvenile	
SNOW GEESE			
BLUE GEESE			

☐ BIRD LEG BAND RECOVERED ON SPECIES:_____

NO. ON BAND: _____

☐ REPORTED TO U.S. F&WS ON DATE _____

RESPONSE: BIRD BAND DATE_____ BANDED WHERE?_____

DATE _____

HUNTING PLACE _____

☐ LAKE   ☐ MARSH   ☐ JUMP SHOOTING ☐ POTHOLES ☐ SHORELAND   ☐ FIELD HUNT

NEAREST CITY _____

DIRECTION FROM CITY: ☐ N   ☐ S   ☐ E   ☐ W   MILES _____

ARRIVAL TIME _____ DEPARTURE TIME _____

HUNTING COMPANIONS: _____
_____
_____

WEATHER: ☐ SUNNY   ☐ PARTLY CLOUDY   ☐ LIGHT OVERCAST   ☐ HEAVY OVERCAST
   ☐ RAIN   ☐ DRIZZLE   ☐ MIST   ☐ FOG   ☐ SLEET   ☐ SNOW

TEMPERATURE: ☐ WARM   ☐ COOL   ☐ COLD   _____ DEGREES

WIND DIRECTION, A.M. _____, P.M. _____ VELOCITY _____ ☐ NO WIND

☐ DECOY SHOOTING   NUMBER OF DECOYS USED: _____ DUCKS _____ GEESE

☐ PASS SHOOTING   CROP RESIDUE (FIELD HUNT) _____

☐ DUCK CALL   ☐ GOOSE CALL   COMMENTS: _____

NOTES: _____
_____
_____
_____
_____
_____
_____
_____
_____

Continued on Next Page

DATE_____

SPECIES BAGGED	NUMBER		COMMENTS
	DRAKES	HENS	
MALLARD			
PINTAIL			
WIDGEON			
GADWALL			
BLUEWING TEAL			
GREENWING TEAL			
SHOVELER			
BLACK DUCK			
WOOD DUCK			
CANVASBACK			
REDHEAD			
BLUEBILL			
RINGBILL			
RUDDY & OTHER			
CANADA GEESE	Greater	Lesser	
WHITE FRONTED GEESE	Adult	Juvenile	
SNOW GEESE			
BLUE GEESE			

☐ BIRD LEG BAND RECOVERED ON SPECIES:_____

NO. ON BAND: _____

☐ REPORTED TO U.S. F&WS ON DATE _____

RESPONSE: BIRD BAND DATE_____ BANDED WHERE?_____

DATE _____

HUNTING PLACE _____

☐ LAKE ☐ MARSH ☐ JUMP SHOOTING ☐ POTHOLES ☐ SHORELAND ☐ FIELD HUNT

NEAREST CITY _____

DIRECTION FROM CITY: ☐ N   ☐ S   ☐ E   ☐ W   MILES _____

ARRIVAL TIME _____ DEPARTURE TIME _____

HUNTING COMPANIONS: _____
_____
_____

WEATHER: ☐ SUNNY   ☐ PARTLY CLOUDY   ☐ LIGHT OVERCAST   ☐ HEAVY OVERCAST
          ☐ RAIN   ☐ DRIZZLE   ☐ MIST   ☐ FOG   ☐ SLEET   ☐ SNOW

TEMPERATURE: ☐ WARM   ☐ COOL   ☐ COLD   _____ DEGREES

WIND DIRECTION, A.M. _____, P.M. _____ VELOCITY _____ ☐ NO WIND

☐ DECOY SHOOTING   NUMBER OF DECOYS USED: _____ DUCKS _____ GEESE

☐ PASS SHOOTING   CROP RESIDUE (FIELD HUNT) _____

☐ DUCK CALL   ☐ GOOSE CALL   COMMENTS: _____

NOTES: _____
_____
_____
_____
_____
_____
_____
_____
_____

Continued on Next Page

DATE_____

SPECIES BAGGED	NUMBER		COMMENTS
	DRAKES	HENS	
MALLARD			
PINTAIL			
WIDGEON			
GADWALL			
BLUEWING TEAL			
GREENWING TEAL			
SHOVELER			
BLACK DUCK			
WOOD DUCK			
CANVASBACK			
REDHEAD			
BLUEBILL			
RINGBILL			
RUDDY & OTHER			
CANADA GEESE	Greater	Lesser	
WHITE FRONTED GEESE	Adult	Juvenile	
SNOW GEESE			
BLUE GEESE			

☐ BIRD LEG BAND RECOVERED ON SPECIES:_____

NO. ON BAND: _____

☐ REPORTED TO U.S. F&WS ON DATE _____

RESPONSE: BIRD BAND DATE_____ BANDED WHERE?_____

DATE _____

HUNTING PLACE _____

☐ LAKE   ☐ MARSH   ☐ JUMP SHOOTING   ☐ POTHOLES   ☐ SHORELAND   ☐ FIELD HUNT

NEAREST CITY _____

DIRECTION FROM CITY: ☐ N   ☐ S   ☐ E   ☐ W   MILES _____

ARRIVAL TIME _____ DEPARTURE TIME _____

HUNTING COMPANIONS: _____
_____
_____

WEATHER: ☐ SUNNY   ☐ PARTLY CLOUDY   ☐ LIGHT OVERCAST   ☐ HEAVY OVERCAST
           ☐ RAIN   ☐ DRIZZLE   ☐ MIST   ☐ FOG   ☐ SLEET   ☐ SNOW

TEMPERATURE: ☐ WARM   ☐ COOL   ☐ COLD   _____ DEGREES

WIND DIRECTION, A.M. _____, P.M. _____   VELOCITY _____   ☐ NO WIND

☐ DECOY SHOOTING   NUMBER OF DECOYS USED: _____ DUCKS _____ GEESE

☐ PASS SHOOTING   CROP RESIDUE (FIELD HUNT) _____

☐ DUCK CALL   ☐ GOOSE CALL   COMMENTS: _____

NOTES: _____
_____
_____
_____
_____
_____
_____
_____

Continued on Next Page

DATE_____

SPECIES BAGGED	NUMBER		COMMENTS
	DRAKES	HENS	
MALLARD			
PINTAIL			
WIDGEON			
GADWALL			
BLUEWING TEAL			
GREENWING TEAL			
SHOVELER			
BLACK DUCK			
WOOD DUCK			
CANVASBACK			
REDHEAD			
BLUEBILL			
RINGBILL			
RUDDY & OTHER			
CANADA GEESE	Greater	Lesser	
WHITE FRONTED GEESE	Adult	Juvenile	
SNOW GEESE			
BLUE GEESE			

☐ BIRD LEG BAND RECOVERED ON SPECIES:_____

NO. ON BAND: _____

☐ REPORTED TO U.S. F&WS ON DATE _____

RESPONSE: BIRD BAND DATE_____ BANDED WHERE?_____

DATE _____

HUNTING PLACE _____

☐ LAKE   ☐ MARSH   ☐ JUMP SHOOTING ☐ POTHOLES ☐ SHORELAND   ☐ FIELD HUNT

NEAREST CITY _____

DIRECTION FROM CITY: ☐ N   ☐ S   ☐ E   ☐ W   MILES _____

ARRIVAL TIME _____ DEPARTURE TIME _____

HUNTING COMPANIONS: _____
_____
_____

WEATHER: ☐ SUNNY   ☐ PARTLY CLOUDY   ☐ LIGHT OVERCAST   ☐ HEAVY OVERCAST
            ☐ RAIN   ☐ DRIZZLE   ☐ MIST   ☐ FOG   ☐ SLEET   ☐ SNOW

TEMPERATURE: ☐ WARM   ☐ COOL   ☐ COLD   _____ DEGREES

WIND DIRECTION, A.M. _____, P.M. _____ VELOCITY _____ ☐ NO WIND

☐ DECOY SHOOTING   NUMBER OF DECOYS USED: _____ DUCKS _____ GEESE

☐ PASS SHOOTING   CROP RESIDUE (FIELD HUNT) _____

☐ DUCK CALL   ☐ GOOSE CALL   COMMENTS: _____

NOTES: _____
_____
_____
_____
_____
_____
_____
_____

Continued on Next Page

DATE_____

SPECIES BAGGED	NUMBER		COMMENTS
	DRAKES	HENS	
MALLARD			
PINTAIL			
WIDGEON			
GADWALL			
BLUEWING TEAL			
GREENWING TEAL			
SHOVELER			
BLACK DUCK			
WOOD DUCK			
CANVASBACK			
REDHEAD			
BLUEBILL			
RINGBILL			
RUDDY & OTHER			
CANADA GEESE	Greater	Lesser	
WHITE FRONTED GEESE	Adult	Juvenile	
SNOW GEESE			
BLUE GEESE			

☐ BIRD LEG BAND RECOVERED ON SPECIES:_____

NO. ON BAND: _____

☐ REPORTED TO U.S. F&WS ON DATE _____

RESPONSE: BIRD BAND DATE_____ BANDED WHERE?_____

DATE _____

HUNTING PLACE _____

☐ LAKE   ☐ MARSH   ☐ JUMP SHOOTING ☐ POTHOLES ☐ SHORELAND   ☐ FIELD HUNT

NEAREST CITY _____

DIRECTION FROM CITY: ☐ N   ☐ S   ☐ E   ☐ W   MILES _____

ARRIVAL TIME _____ DEPARTURE TIME _____

HUNTING COMPANIONS: _____

_____

_____

WEATHER: ☐ SUNNY   ☐ PARTLY CLOUDY   ☐ LIGHT OVERCAST   ☐ HEAVY OVERCAST

☐ RAIN   ☐ DRIZZLE   ☐ MIST   ☐ FOG   ☐ SLEET   ☐ SNOW

TEMPERATURE: ☐ WARM   ☐ COOL   ☐ COLD   _____ DEGREES

WIND DIRECTION, A.M._____, P.M._____ VELOCITY_____ ☐ NO WIND

☐ DECOY SHOOTING   NUMBER OF DECOYS USED:_____ DUCKS _____ GEESE

☐ PASS SHOOTING   CROP RESIDUE (FIELD HUNT) _____

☐ DUCK CALL   ☐ GOOSE CALL   COMMENTS: _____

NOTES: _____

_____

_____

_____

_____

_____

_____

_____

Continued on Next Page

DATE_____

SPECIES BAGGED	NUMBER		COMMENTS
	DRAKES	HENS	
MALLARD			
PINTAIL			
WIDGEON			
GADWALL			
BLUEWING TEAL			
GREENWING TEAL			
SHOVELER			
BLACK DUCK			
WOOD DUCK			
CANVASBACK			
REDHEAD			
BLUEBILL			
RINGBILL			
RUDDY & OTHER			
CANADA GEESE	Greater	Lesser	
WHITE FRONTED GEESE	Adult	Juvenile	
SNOW GEESE			
BLUE GEESE			

☐ BIRD LEG BAND RECOVERED ON SPECIES:_____

NO. ON BAND: _____

☐ REPORTED TO U.S. F&WS ON DATE _____

RESPONSE: BIRD BAND DATE_____ BANDED WHERE?_____

DATE _____

HUNTING PLACE _____

☐ LAKE ☐ MARSH ☐ JUMP SHOOTING ☐ POTHOLES ☐ SHORELAND ☐ FIELD HUNT

NEAREST CITY _____

DIRECTION FROM CITY: ☐ N ☐ S ☐ E ☐ W MILES _____

ARRIVAL TIME _____ DEPARTURE TIME _____

HUNTING COMPANIONS: _____

_____

_____

WEATHER: ☐ SUNNY ☐ PARTLY CLOUDY ☐ LIGHT OVERCAST ☐ HEAVY OVERCAST
☐ RAIN ☐ DRIZZLE ☐ MIST ☐ FOG ☐ SLEET ☐ SNOW

TEMPERATURE: ☐ WARM ☐ COOL ☐ COLD _____ DEGREES

WIND DIRECTION, A.M. _____, P.M. _____ VELOCITY _____ ☐ NO WIND

☐ DECOY SHOOTING NUMBER OF DECOYS USED: _____ DUCKS _____ GEESE

☐ PASS SHOOTING CROP RESIDUE (FIELD HUNT) _____

☐ DUCK CALL ☐ GOOSE CALL COMMENTS: _____

NOTES: _____

_____

_____

_____

_____

_____

_____

_____

_____

Continued on Next Page

DATE_____

SPECIES BAGGED	NUMBER		COMMENTS
	DRAKES	HENS	
MALLARD			
PINTAIL			
WIDGEON			
GADWALL			
BLUEWING TEAL			
GREENWING TEAL			
SHOVELER			
BLACK DUCK			
WOOD DUCK			
CANVASBACK			
REDHEAD			
BLUEBILL			
RINGBILL			
RUDDY & OTHER			
CANADA GEESE	Greater	Lesser	
WHITE FRONTED GEESE	Adult	Juvenile	
SNOW GEESE			
BLUE GEESE			

☐ BIRD LEG BAND RECOVERED ON SPECIES:_____

NO. ON BAND: _____

☐ REPORTED TO U.S. F&WS ON DATE _____

RESPONSE: BIRD BAND DATE_____ BANDED WHERE?_____

DATE _____

HUNTING PLACE _____

☐ LAKE   ☐ MARSH   ☐ JUMP SHOOTING   ☐ POTHOLES   ☐ SHORELAND   ☐ FIELD HUNT

NEAREST CITY _____

DIRECTION FROM CITY: ☐ N   ☐ S   ☐ E   ☐ W   MILES _____

ARRIVAL TIME _____ DEPARTURE TIME _____

HUNTING COMPANIONS: _____
_____
_____

WEATHER: ☐ SUNNY   ☐ PARTLY CLOUDY   ☐ LIGHT OVERCAST   ☐ HEAVY OVERCAST
           ☐ RAIN   ☐ DRIZZLE   ☐ MIST   ☐ FOG   ☐ SLEET   ☐ SNOW

TEMPERATURE: ☐ WARM   ☐ COOL   ☐ COLD   _____ DEGREES

WIND DIRECTION, A.M. _____, P.M. _____ VELOCITY _____ ☐ NO WIND

☐ DECOY SHOOTING   NUMBER OF DECOYS USED: _____ DUCKS _____ GEESE

☐ PASS SHOOTING   CROP RESIDUE (FIELD HUNT) _____

☐ DUCK CALL   ☐ GOOSE CALL   COMMENTS: _____

NOTES: _____
_____
_____
_____
_____
_____
_____
_____
_____

Continued on Next Page

DATE_____

SPECIES BAGGED	NUMBER		COMMENTS
	DRAKES	HENS	
MALLARD			
PINTAIL			
WIDGEON			
GADWALL			
BLUEWING TEAL			
GREENWING TEAL			
SHOVELER			
BLACK DUCK			
WOOD DUCK			
CANVASBACK			
REDHEAD			
BLUEBILL			
RINGBILL			
RUDDY & OTHER			
CANADA GEESE	Greater	Lesser	
WHITE FRONTED GEESE	Adult	Juvenile	
SNOW GEESE			
BLUE GEESE			

☐ BIRD LEG BAND RECOVERED ON SPECIES:_____

NO. ON BAND: _____

☐ REPORTED TO U.S. F&WS ON DATE _____

RESPONSE: BIRD BAND DATE_____ BANDED WHERE?_____

DATE _____

HUNTING PLACE _____

☐ LAKE   ☐ MARSH   ☐ JUMP SHOOTING ☐ POTHOLES ☐ SHORELAND   ☐ FIELD HUNT

NEAREST CITY _____

DIRECTION FROM CITY: ☐ N   ☐ S   ☐ E   ☐ W   MILES _____

ARRIVAL TIME _____ DEPARTURE TIME _____

HUNTING COMPANIONS: _____
_____
_____

WEATHER: ☐ SUNNY   ☐ PARTLY CLOUDY   ☐ LIGHT OVERCAST   ☐ HEAVY OVERCAST
           ☐ RAIN   ☐ DRIZZLE   ☐ MIST   ☐ FOG   ☐ SLEET   ☐ SNOW

TEMPERATURE: ☐ WARM   ☐ COOL   ☐ COLD   _____ DEGREES

WIND DIRECTION, A.M. _____, P.M. _____ VELOCITY _____ ☐ NO WIND

☐ DECOY SHOOTING   NUMBER OF DECOYS USED: _____ DUCKS _____ GEESE

☐ PASS SHOOTING   CROP RESIDUE (FIELD HUNT) _____

☐ DUCK CALL   ☐ GOOSE CALL   COMMENTS: _____

NOTES: _____
_____
_____
_____
_____
_____
_____
_____
_____

Continued on Next Page

DATE_____

SPECIES BAGGED	NUMBER		COMMENTS
	DRAKES	HENS	
MALLARD			
PINTAIL			
WIDGEON			
GADWALL			
BLUEWING TEAL			
GREENWING TEAL			
SHOVELER			
BLACK DUCK			
WOOD DUCK			
CANVASBACK			
REDHEAD			
BLUEBILL			
RINGBILL			
RUDDY & OTHER			
CANADA GEESE	Greater	Lesser	
WHITE FRONTED GEESE	Adult	Juvenile	
SNOW GEESE			
BLUE GEESE			

☐ BIRD LEG BAND RECOVERED ON SPECIES:_____

NO. ON BAND: _____

☐ REPORTED TO U.S. F&WS ON DATE _____

RESPONSE: BIRD BAND DATE_____ BANDED WHERE?_____

DATE _____

HUNTING PLACE _____

☐ LAKE   ☐ MARSH   ☐ JUMP SHOOTING ☐ POTHOLES ☐ SHORELAND   ☐ FIELD HUNT

NEAREST CITY _____

DIRECTION FROM CITY: ☐ N   ☐ S   ☐ E   ☐ W   MILES _____

ARRIVAL TIME _____ DEPARTURE TIME _____

HUNTING COMPANIONS: _____
_____
_____

WEATHER: ☐ SUNNY   ☐ PARTLY CLOUDY   ☐ LIGHT OVERCAST   ☐ HEAVY OVERCAST
           ☐ RAIN   ☐ DRIZZLE   ☐ MIST   ☐ FOG   ☐ SLEET   ☐ SNOW

TEMPERATURE: ☐ WARM   ☐ COOL   ☐ COLD   _____ DEGREES

WIND DIRECTION, A.M. _____, P.M. _____ VELOCITY _____ ☐ NO WIND

☐ DECOY SHOOTING   NUMBER OF DECOYS USED: _____ DUCKS _____ GEESE

☐ PASS SHOOTING   CROP RESIDUE (FIELD HUNT) _____

☐ DUCK CALL   ☐ GOOSE CALL   COMMENTS: _____

NOTES: _____
_____
_____
_____
_____
_____
_____
_____

Continued on Next Page

DATE_____

SPECIES BAGGED	NUMBER		COMMENTS
	DRAKES	HENS	
MALLARD			
PINTAIL			
WIDGEON			
GADWALL			
BLUEWING TEAL			
GREENWING TEAL			
SHOVELER			
BLACK DUCK			
WOOD DUCK			
CANVASBACK			
REDHEAD			
BLUEBILL			
RINGBILL			
RUDDY & OTHER			
CANADA GEESE	Greater	Lesser	
WHITE FRONTED GEESE	Adult	Juvenile	
SNOW GEESE			
BLUE GEESE			

☐ BIRD LEG BAND RECOVERED ON SPECIES:_____

NO. ON BAND: _____

☐ REPORTED TO U.S. F&WS ON DATE _____

RESPONSE: BIRD BAND DATE_____ BANDED WHERE?_____

DATE _____

HUNTING PLACE _____

☐ LAKE   ☐ MARSH   ☐ JUMP SHOOTING ☐ POTHOLES ☐ SHORELAND   ☐ FIELD HUNT

NEAREST CITY _____

DIRECTION FROM CITY: ☐ N   ☐ S   ☐ E   ☐ W   MILES _____

ARRIVAL TIME _____ DEPARTURE TIME _____

HUNTING COMPANIONS: _____

_____

_____

WEATHER: ☐ SUNNY   ☐ PARTLY CLOUDY   ☐ LIGHT OVERCAST   ☐ HEAVY OVERCAST

   ☐ RAIN   ☐ DRIZZLE   ☐ MIST   ☐ FOG   ☐ SLEET   ☐ SNOW

TEMPERATURE: ☐ WARM   ☐ COOL   ☐ COLD   _____ DEGREES

WIND DIRECTION, A.M. _____, P.M. _____ VELOCITY _____ ☐ NO WIND

☐ DECOY SHOOTING   NUMBER OF DECOYS USED: _____ DUCKS _____ GEESE

☐ PASS SHOOTING   CROP RESIDUE (FIELD HUNT) _____

☐ DUCK CALL   ☐ GOOSE CALL   COMMENTS: _____

NOTES: _____

_____

_____

_____

_____

_____

_____

_____

Continued on Next Page

DATE_____

SPECIES BAGGED	NUMBER		COMMENTS
	DRAKES	HENS	
MALLARD			
PINTAIL			
WIDGEON			
GADWALL			
BLUEWING TEAL			
GREENWING TEAL			
SHOVELER			
BLACK DUCK			
WOOD DUCK			
CANVASBACK			
REDHEAD			
BLUEBILL			
RINGBILL			
RUDDY & OTHER			
CANADA GEESE	**Greater**	**Lesser**	
WHITE FRONTED GEESE	**Adult**	**Juvenile**	
SNOW GEESE			
BLUE GEESE			

☐ BIRD LEG BAND RECOVERED ON SPECIES:_____

NO. ON BAND: _____

☐ REPORTED TO U.S. F&WS ON DATE _____

RESPONSE: BIRD BAND DATE_____ BANDED WHERE?_____

DATE _____

HUNTING PLACE _____

☐ LAKE   ☐ MARSH   ☐ JUMP SHOOTING ☐ POTHOLES ☐ SHORELAND   ☐ FIELD HUNT

NEAREST CITY _____

DIRECTION FROM CITY: ☐ N   ☐ S   ☐ E   ☐ W   MILES _____

ARRIVAL TIME _____ DEPARTURE TIME _____

HUNTING COMPANIONS: _____
_____
_____

WEATHER: ☐ SUNNY   ☐ PARTLY CLOUDY   ☐ LIGHT OVERCAST   ☐ HEAVY OVERCAST
           ☐ RAIN   ☐ DRIZZLE   ☐ MIST   ☐ FOG   ☐ SLEET   ☐ SNOW

TEMPERATURE: ☐ WARM   ☐ COOL   ☐ COLD   _____ DEGREES

WIND DIRECTION, A.M. _____, P.M. _____ VELOCITY _____   ☐ NO WIND

☐ DECOY SHOOTING   NUMBER OF DECOYS USED: _____ DUCKS _____ GEESE

☐ PASS SHOOTING   CROP RESIDUE (FIELD HUNT) _____

☐ DUCK CALL   ☐ GOOSE CALL   COMMENTS: _____

NOTES: _____
_____
_____
_____
_____
_____
_____
_____
_____

Continued on Next Page

DATE_____

SPECIES BAGGED	NUMBER		COMMENTS
	DRAKES	HENS	
MALLARD			
PINTAIL			
WIDGEON			
GADWALL			
BLUEWING TEAL			
GREENWING TEAL			
SHOVELER			
BLACK DUCK			
WOOD DUCK			
CANVASBACK			
REDHEAD			
BLUEBILL			
RINGBILL			
RUDDY & OTHER			
CANADA GEESE	Greater	Lesser	
WHITE FRONTED GEESE	Adult	Juvenile	
SNOW GEESE			
BLUE GEESE			

☐ BIRD LEG BAND RECOVERED ON SPECIES:_____

NO. ON BAND: _____

☐ REPORTED TO U.S. F&WS ON DATE _____

RESPONSE: BIRD BAND DATE_____ BANDED WHERE?_____

DATE _____

HUNTING PLACE _____

☐ LAKE ☐ MARSH ☐ JUMP SHOOTING ☐ POTHOLES ☐ SHORELAND ☐ FIELD HUNT

NEAREST CITY _____

DIRECTION FROM CITY: ☐ N ☐ S ☐ E ☐ W MILES _____

ARRIVAL TIME _____ DEPARTURE TIME _____

HUNTING COMPANIONS: _____
_____
_____

WEATHER: ☐ SUNNY ☐ PARTLY CLOUDY ☐ LIGHT OVERCAST ☐ HEAVY OVERCAST
          ☐ RAIN ☐ DRIZZLE ☐ MIST ☐ FOG ☐ SLEET ☐ SNOW

TEMPERATURE: ☐ WARM ☐ COOL ☐ COLD _____ DEGREES

WIND DIRECTION, A.M. _____, P.M. _____ VELOCITY _____ ☐ NO WIND

☐ DECOY SHOOTING   NUMBER OF DECOYS USED: _____ DUCKS _____ GEESE

☐ PASS SHOOTING   CROP RESIDUE (FIELD HUNT) _____

☐ DUCK CALL   ☐ GOOSE CALL   COMMENTS: _____

NOTES: _____
_____
_____
_____
_____
_____
_____
_____
_____

Continued on Next Page

DATE_____

SPECIES BAGGED	NUMBER		COMMENTS
	DRAKES	HENS	
MALLARD			
PINTAIL			
WIDGEON			
GADWALL			
BLUEWING TEAL			
GREENWING TEAL			
SHOVELER			
BLACK DUCK			
WOOD DUCK			
CANVASBACK			
REDHEAD			
BLUEBILL			
RINGBILL			
RUDDY & OTHER			
CANADA GEESE	Greater	Lesser	
WHITE FRONTED GEESE	Adult	Juvenile	
SNOW GEESE			
BLUE GEESE			

☐ BIRD LEG BAND RECOVERED ON SPECIES:_____

NO. ON BAND: _____

☐ REPORTED TO U.S. F&WS ON DATE _____

RESPONSE: BIRD BAND DATE_____ BANDED WHERE?_____

DATE _____

HUNTING PLACE _____

☐ LAKE   ☐ MARSH   ☐ JUMP SHOOTING ☐ POTHOLES ☐ SHORELAND   ☐ FIELD HUNT

NEAREST CITY _____

DIRECTION FROM CITY: ☐ N   ☐ S   ☐ E   ☐ W   MILES _____

ARRIVAL TIME _____ DEPARTURE TIME _____

HUNTING COMPANIONS: _____

_____

_____

WEATHER: ☐ SUNNY   ☐ PARTLY CLOUDY   ☐ LIGHT OVERCAST   ☐ HEAVY OVERCAST
           ☐ RAIN   ☐ DRIZZLE   ☐ MIST   ☐ FOG   ☐ SLEET   ☐ SNOW

TEMPERATURE: ☐ WARM   ☐ COOL   ☐ COLD   _____ DEGREES

WIND DIRECTION, A.M. _____, P.M. _____   VELOCITY _____   ☐ NO WIND

☐ DECOY SHOOTING   NUMBER OF DECOYS USED: _____ DUCKS _____ GEESE

☐ PASS SHOOTING   CROP RESIDUE (FIELD HUNT) _____

☐ DUCK CALL   ☐ GOOSE CALL   COMMENTS: _____

NOTES: _____

_____

_____

_____

_____

_____

_____

_____

_____

Continued on Next Page

DATE_____

SPECIES BAGGED	NUMBER		COMMENTS
	DRAKES	HENS	
MALLARD			
PINTAIL			
WIDGEON			
GADWALL			
BLUEWING TEAL			
GREENWING TEAL			
SHOVELER			
BLACK DUCK			
WOOD DUCK			
CANVASBACK			
REDHEAD			
BLUEBILL			
RINGBILL			
RUDDY & OTHER			
CANADA GEESE	Greater	Lesser	
WHITE FRONTED GEESE	Adult	Juvenile	
SNOW GEESE			
BLUE GEESE			

☐ BIRD LEG BAND RECOVERED ON SPECIES:_____

NO. ON BAND: _____

☐ REPORTED TO U.S. F&WS ON DATE _____

RESPONSE: BIRD BAND DATE_____ BANDED WHERE?_____

DATE _____

HUNTING PLACE _____

☐ LAKE   ☐ MARSH   ☐ JUMP SHOOTING   ☐ POTHOLES   ☐ SHORELAND   ☐ FIELD HUNT

NEAREST CITY _____

DIRECTION FROM CITY: ☐ N   ☐ S   ☐ E   ☐ W   MILES _____

ARRIVAL TIME _____ DEPARTURE TIME _____

HUNTING COMPANIONS: _____
_____
_____

WEATHER: ☐ SUNNY   ☐ PARTLY CLOUDY   ☐ LIGHT OVERCAST   ☐ HEAVY OVERCAST
           ☐ RAIN   ☐ DRIZZLE   ☐ MIST   ☐ FOG   ☐ SLEET   ☐ SNOW

TEMPERATURE: ☐ WARM   ☐ COOL   ☐ COLD   _____DEGREES

WIND DIRECTION, A.M. _____, P.M. _____ VELOCITY _____ ☐ NO WIND

☐ DECOY SHOOTING   NUMBER OF DECOYS USED: _____ DUCKS _____ GEESE

☐ PASS SHOOTING   CROP RESIDUE (FIELD HUNT) _____

☐ DUCK CALL   ☐ GOOSE CALL   COMMENTS: _____

NOTES: _____
_____
_____
_____
_____
_____
_____
_____
_____

Continued on Next Page

DATE_____

SPECIES BAGGED	NUMBER		COMMENTS
	DRAKES	HENS	
MALLARD			
PINTAIL			
WIDGEON			
GADWALL			
BLUEWING TEAL			
GREENWING TEAL			
SHOVELER			
BLACK DUCK			
WOOD DUCK			
CANVASBACK			
REDHEAD			
BLUEBILL			
RINGBILL			
RUDDY & OTHER			
CANADA GEESE	Greater	Lesser	
WHITE FRONTED GEESE	Adult	Juvenile	
SNOW GEESE			
BLUE GEESE			

☐ BIRD LEG BAND RECOVERED ON SPECIES:_____

NO. ON BAND: _____

☐ REPORTED TO U.S. F&WS ON DATE _____

RESPONSE: BIRD BAND DATE_____ BANDED WHERE?_____

DATE _____

HUNTING PLACE _____

☐ LAKE   ☐ MARSH   ☐ JUMP SHOOTING ☐ POTHOLES ☐ SHORELAND   ☐ FIELD HUNT

NEAREST CITY _____

DIRECTION FROM CITY: ☐ N   ☐ S   ☐ E   ☐ W   MILES _____

ARRIVAL TIME _____ DEPARTURE TIME _____

HUNTING COMPANIONS: _____
_____
_____

WEATHER: ☐ SUNNY   ☐ PARTLY CLOUDY   ☐ LIGHT OVERCAST   ☐ HEAVY OVERCAST
           ☐ RAIN   ☐ DRIZZLE   ☐ MIST   ☐ FOG   ☐ SLEET   ☐ SNOW

TEMPERATURE: ☐ WARM   ☐ COOL   ☐ COLD   _____ DEGREES

WIND DIRECTION, A.M. _____, P.M. _____ VELOCITY _____ ☐ NO WIND

☐ DECOY SHOOTING   NUMBER OF DECOYS USED: _____ DUCKS _____ GEESE

☐ PASS SHOOTING   CROP RESIDUE (FIELD HUNT) _____

☐ DUCK CALL   ☐ GOOSE CALL   COMMENTS: _____

NOTES: _____
_____
_____
_____
_____
_____
_____
_____
_____

Continued on Next Page

DATE_____

SPECIES BAGGED	NUMBER		COMMENTS
	DRAKES	HENS	
MALLARD			
PINTAIL			
WIDGEON			
GADWALL			
BLUEWING TEAL			
GREENWING TEAL			
SHOVELER			
BLACK DUCK			
WOOD DUCK			
CANVASBACK			
REDHEAD			
BLUEBILL			
RINGBILL			
RUDDY & OTHER			
CANADA GEESE	Greater	Lesser	
WHITE FRONTED GEESE	Adult	Juvenile	
SNOW GEESE			
BLUE GEESE			

☐ BIRD LEG BAND RECOVERED ON SPECIES:_____

NO. ON BAND: _____

☐ REPORTED TO U.S. F&WS ON DATE _____

RESPONSE: BIRD BAND DATE_____ BANDED WHERE?_____

DATE _____

HUNTING PLACE _____

☐ LAKE   ☐ MARSH   ☐ JUMP SHOOTING ☐ POTHOLES ☐ SHORELAND   ☐ FIELD HUNT

NEAREST CITY _____

DIRECTION FROM CITY: ☐ N   ☐ S   ☐ E   ☐ W   MILES _____

ARRIVAL TIME _____ DEPARTURE TIME _____

HUNTING COMPANIONS: _____
_____
_____

WEATHER: ☐ SUNNY   ☐ PARTLY CLOUDY   ☐ LIGHT OVERCAST   ☐ HEAVY OVERCAST
           ☐ RAIN   ☐ DRIZZLE   ☐ MIST   ☐ FOG   ☐ SLEET   ☐ SNOW

TEMPERATURE: ☐ WARM   ☐ COOL   ☐ COLD   _____ DEGREES

WIND DIRECTION, A.M. _____, P.M. _____ VELOCITY _____   ☐ NO WIND

☐ DECOY SHOOTING   NUMBER OF DECOYS USED: _____ DUCKS _____ GEESE

☐ PASS SHOOTING   CROP RESIDUE (FIELD HUNT) _____

☐ DUCK CALL   ☐ GOOSE CALL   COMMENTS: _____

NOTES: _____
_____
_____
_____
_____
_____
_____
_____
_____

Continued on Next Page

DATE _____

SPECIES BAGGED	NUMBER		COMMENTS
	DRAKES	HENS	
MALLARD			
PINTAIL			
WIDGEON			
GADWALL			
BLUEWING TEAL			
GREENWING TEAL			
SHOVELER			
BLACK DUCK			
WOOD DUCK			
CANVASBACK			
REDHEAD			
BLUEBILL			
RINGBILL			
RUDDY & OTHER			
CANADA GEESE	Greater	Lesser	
WHITE FRONTED GEESE	Adult	Juvenile	
SNOW GEESE			
BLUE GEESE			

☐ BIRD LEG BAND RECOVERED ON SPECIES:_____

NO. ON BAND: _____

☐ REPORTED TO U.S. F&WS ON DATE _____

RESPONSE: BIRD BAND DATE_____ BANDED WHERE?_____

DATE _____

HUNTING PLACE _____

☐ LAKE   ☐ MARSH   ☐ JUMP SHOOTING   ☐ POTHOLES   ☐ SHORELAND   ☐ FIELD HUNT

NEAREST CITY _____

DIRECTION FROM CITY: ☐ N   ☐ S   ☐ E   ☐ W   MILES _____

ARRIVAL TIME _____ DEPARTURE TIME _____

HUNTING COMPANIONS: _____
_____
_____

WEATHER: ☐ SUNNY   ☐ PARTLY CLOUDY   ☐ LIGHT OVERCAST   ☐ HEAVY OVERCAST
           ☐ RAIN   ☐ DRIZZLE   ☐ MIST   ☐ FOG   ☐ SLEET   ☐ SNOW

TEMPERATURE: ☐ WARM   ☐ COOL   ☐ COLD   _____ DEGREES

WIND DIRECTION, A.M. _____, P.M. _____   VELOCITY _____   ☐ NO WIND

☐ DECOY SHOOTING   NUMBER OF DECOYS USED: _____ DUCKS _____ GEESE

☐ PASS SHOOTING   CROP RESIDUE (FIELD HUNT) _____

☐ DUCK CALL   ☐ GOOSE CALL   COMMENTS: _____

NOTES: _____
_____
_____
_____
_____
_____
_____
_____

DATE _____

SPECIES BAGGED	NUMBER		COMMENTS
	DRAKES	HENS	
MALLARD			
PINTAIL			
WIDGEON			
GADWALL			
BLUEWING TEAL			
GREENWING TEAL			
SHOVELER			
BLACK DUCK			
WOOD DUCK			
CANVASBACK			
REDHEAD			
BLUEBILL			
RINGBILL			
RUDDY & OTHER			
CANADA GEESE	Greater	Lesser	
WHITE FRONTED GEESE	Adult	Juvenile	
SNOW GEESE			
BLUE GEESE			

☐ BIRD LEG BAND RECOVERED ON SPECIES: _____

NO. ON BAND: _____

☐ REPORTED TO U.S. F&WS ON DATE _____

RESPONSE: BIRD BAND DATE _____ BANDED WHERE? _____

DATE _____

HUNTING PLACE _____

☐ LAKE   ☐ MARSH   ☐ JUMP SHOOTING ☐ POTHOLES ☐ SHORELAND   ☐ FIELD HUNT

NEAREST CITY _____

DIRECTION FROM CITY: ☐ N   ☐ S   ☐ E   ☐ W   MILES _____

ARRIVAL TIME _____ DEPARTURE TIME _____

HUNTING COMPANIONS: _____
_____
_____

WEATHER: ☐ SUNNY   ☐ PARTLY CLOUDY   ☐ LIGHT OVERCAST   ☐ HEAVY OVERCAST

☐ RAIN   ☐ DRIZZLE   ☐ MIST   ☐ FOG   ☐ SLEET   ☐ SNOW

TEMPERATURE: ☐ WARM   ☐ COOL   ☐ COLD   _____DEGREES

WIND DIRECTION, A.M._____, P.M._____ VELOCITY_____ ☐ NO WIND

☐ DECOY SHOOTING   NUMBER OF DECOYS USED:_____DUCKS _____GEESE

☐ PASS SHOOTING   CROP RESIDUE (FIELD HUNT) _____

☐ DUCK CALL   ☐ GOOSE CALL   COMMENTS: _____

NOTES: _____
_____
_____
_____
_____
_____
_____
_____

Continued on Next Page

DATE_____

SPECIES BAGGED	NUMBER		COMMENTS
	DRAKES	HENS	
MALLARD			
PINTAIL			
WIDGEON			
GADWALL			
BLUEWING TEAL			
GREENWING TEAL			
SHOVELER			
BLACK DUCK			
WOOD DUCK			
CANVASBACK			
REDHEAD			
BLUEBILL			
RINGBILL			
RUDDY & OTHER			
CANADA GEESE	Greater	Lesser	
WHITE FRONTED GEESE	Adult	Juvenile	
SNOW GEESE			
BLUE GEESE			

☐ BIRD LEG BAND RECOVERED ON SPECIES:_____

NO. ON BAND: _____

☐ REPORTED TO U.S. F&WS ON DATE _____

RESPONSE: BIRD BAND DATE_____ BANDED WHERE?_____

DATE _____

HUNTING PLACE _____

☐ LAKE   ☐ MARSH   ☐ JUMP SHOOTING ☐ POTHOLES ☐ SHORELAND   ☐ FIELD HUNT

NEAREST CITY _____

DIRECTION FROM CITY: ☐ N   ☐ S   ☐ E   ☐ W   MILES _____

ARRIVAL TIME _____ DEPARTURE TIME _____

HUNTING COMPANIONS: _____
_____
_____

WEATHER: ☐ SUNNY   ☐ PARTLY CLOUDY   ☐ LIGHT OVERCAST   ☐ HEAVY OVERCAST

☐ RAIN   ☐ DRIZZLE   ☐ MIST   ☐ FOG   ☐ SLEET   ☐ SNOW

TEMPERATURE: ☐ WARM   ☐ COOL   ☐ COLD   _____ DEGREES

WIND DIRECTION, A.M._____, P.M._____ VELOCITY_____   ☐ NO WIND

☐ DECOY SHOOTING   NUMBER OF DECOYS USED:_____ DUCKS _____ GEESE

☐ PASS SHOOTING   CROP RESIDUE (FIELD HUNT) _____

☐ DUCK CALL   ☐ GOOSE CALL   COMMENTS: _____

NOTES: _____
_____
_____
_____
_____
_____
_____
_____
_____

Continued on Next Page

DATE_____

SPECIES BAGGED	NUMBER		COMMENTS
	DRAKES	HENS	
MALLARD			
PINTAIL			
WIDGEON			
GADWALL			
BLUEWING TEAL			
GREENWING TEAL			
SHOVELER			
BLACK DUCK			
WOOD DUCK			
CANVASBACK			
REDHEAD			
BLUEBILL			
RINGBILL			
RUDDY & OTHER			
CANADA GEESE	**Greater**	**Lesser**	
WHITE FRONTED GEESE	**Adult**	**Juvenile**	
SNOW GEESE			
BLUE GEESE			

☐ BIRD LEG BAND RECOVERED ON SPECIES:_____

NO. ON BAND: _____

☐ REPORTED TO U.S. F&WS ON DATE _____

RESPONSE: BIRD BAND DATE_____ BANDED WHERE?_____

DATE _____

HUNTING PLACE _____

☐ LAKE   ☐ MARSH   ☐ JUMP SHOOTING ☐ POTHOLES ☐ SHORELAND   ☐ FIELD HUNT

NEAREST CITY _____

DIRECTION FROM CITY: ☐ N   ☐ S   ☐ E   ☐ W   MILES _____

ARRIVAL TIME _____ DEPARTURE TIME _____

HUNTING COMPANIONS: _____
_____
_____

WEATHER: ☐ SUNNY   ☐ PARTLY CLOUDY   ☐ LIGHT OVERCAST   ☐ HEAVY OVERCAST
           ☐ RAIN   ☐ DRIZZLE   ☐ MIST   ☐ FOG   ☐ SLEET   ☐ SNOW

TEMPERATURE: ☐ WARM   ☐ COOL   ☐ COLD   _____ DEGREES

WIND DIRECTION, A.M. _____, P.M. _____ VELOCITY _____ ☐ NO WIND

☐ DECOY SHOOTING   NUMBER OF DECOYS USED: _____ DUCKS _____ GEESE

☐ PASS SHOOTING   CROP RESIDUE (FIELD HUNT) _____

☐ DUCK CALL   ☐ GOOSE CALL   COMMENTS: _____

NOTES: _____
_____
_____
_____
_____
_____
_____
_____

Continued on Next Page

DATE_____

SPECIES BAGGED	NUMBER		COMMENTS
	DRAKES	HENS	
MALLARD			
PINTAIL			
WIDGEON			
GADWALL			
BLUEWING TEAL			
GREENWING TEAL			
SHOVELER			
BLACK DUCK			
WOOD DUCK			
CANVASBACK			
REDHEAD			
BLUEBILL			
RINGBILL			
RUDDY & OTHER			
CANADA GEESE	Greater	Lesser	
WHITE FRONTED GEESE	Adult	Juvenile	
SNOW GEESE			
BLUE GEESE			

☐ BIRD LEG BAND RECOVERED ON SPECIES:_____

NO. ON BAND: _____

☐ REPORTED TO U.S. F&WS ON DATE _____

RESPONSE: BIRD BAND DATE_____ BANDED WHERE?_____

DATE _____

HUNTING PLACE _____

☐ LAKE   ☐ MARSH   ☐ JUMP SHOOTING ☐ POTHOLES ☐ SHORELAND   ☐ FIELD HUNT

NEAREST CITY _____

DIRECTION FROM CITY: ☐ N   ☐ S   ☐ E   ☐ W   MILES _____

ARRIVAL TIME _____ DEPARTURE TIME _____

HUNTING COMPANIONS: _____
_____
_____

WEATHER: ☐ SUNNY   ☐ PARTLY CLOUDY   ☐ LIGHT OVERCAST   ☐ HEAVY OVERCAST
           ☐ RAIN   ☐ DRIZZLE   ☐ MIST   ☐ FOG   ☐ SLEET   ☐ SNOW

TEMPERATURE: ☐ WARM   ☐ COOL   ☐ COLD   _____ DEGREES

WIND DIRECTION, A.M. _____, P.M. _____ VELOCITY _____ ☐ NO WIND

☐ DECOY SHOOTING   NUMBER OF DECOYS USED: _____ DUCKS _____ GEESE

☐ PASS SHOOTING   CROP RESIDUE (FIELD HUNT) _____

☐ DUCK CALL   ☐ GOOSE CALL   COMMENTS: _____

NOTES: _____
_____
_____
_____
_____
_____
_____
_____
_____

Continued on Next Page

DATE_____

SPECIES BAGGED	NUMBER		COMMENTS
	DRAKES	HENS	
MALLARD			
PINTAIL			
WIDGEON			
GADWALL			
BLUEWING TEAL			
GREENWING TEAL			
SHOVELER			
BLACK DUCK			
WOOD DUCK			
CANVASBACK			
REDHEAD			
BLUEBILL			
RINGBILL			
RUDDY & OTHER			
CANADA GEESE	Greater	Lesser	
WHITE FRONTED GEESE	Adult	Juvenile	
SNOW GEESE			
BLUE GEESE			

☐ BIRD LEG BAND RECOVERED ON SPECIES:_____

NO. ON BAND: _____

☐ REPORTED TO U.S. F&WS ON DATE _____

RESPONSE: BIRD BAND DATE_____ BANDED WHERE?_____

DATE _____

HUNTING PLACE _____

☐ LAKE   ☐ MARSH   ☐ JUMP SHOOTING ☐ POTHOLES ☐ SHORELAND   ☐ FIELD HUNT

NEAREST CITY _____

DIRECTION FROM CITY: ☐ N   ☐ S   ☐ E   ☐ W   MILES _____

ARRIVAL TIME _____ DEPARTURE TIME _____

HUNTING COMPANIONS: _____
_____
_____

WEATHER: ☐ SUNNY   ☐ PARTLY CLOUDY   ☐ LIGHT OVERCAST   ☐ HEAVY OVERCAST
            ☐ RAIN   ☐ DRIZZLE   ☐ MIST   ☐ FOG   ☐ SLEET   ☐ SNOW

TEMPERATURE: ☐ WARM   ☐ COOL   ☐ COLD   _____ DEGREES

WIND DIRECTION, A.M. _____, P.M. _____   VELOCITY _____   ☐ NO WIND

☐ DECOY SHOOTING   NUMBER OF DECOYS USED: _____ DUCKS _____ GEESE

☐ PASS SHOOTING   CROP RESIDUE (FIELD HUNT) _____

☐ DUCK CALL   ☐ GOOSE CALL   COMMENTS: _____

NOTES: _____
_____
_____
_____
_____
_____
_____
_____
_____

DATE_____

SPECIES BAGGED	NUMBER		COMMENTS
	DRAKES	HENS	
MALLARD			
PINTAIL			
WIDGEON			
GADWALL			
BLUEWING TEAL			
GREENWING TEAL			
SHOVELER			
BLACK DUCK			
WOOD DUCK			
CANVASBACK			
REDHEAD			
BLUEBILL			
RINGBILL			
RUDDY & OTHER			
CANADA GEESE	Greater	Lesser	
WHITE FRONTED GEESE	Adult	Juvenile	
SNOW GEESE			
BLUE GEESE			

☐ BIRD LEG BAND RECOVERED ON SPECIES:_____

NO. ON BAND: _____

☐ REPORTED TO U.S. F&WS ON DATE _____

RESPONSE: BIRD BAND DATE_____ BANDED WHERE?_____

DATE _____

HUNTING PLACE _____

☐ LAKE   ☐ MARSH   ☐ JUMP SHOOTING ☐ POTHOLES ☐ SHORELAND   ☐ FIELD HUNT

NEAREST CITY _____

DIRECTION FROM CITY: ☐ N   ☐ S   ☐ E   ☐ W   MILES _____

ARRIVAL TIME _____ DEPARTURE TIME _____

HUNTING COMPANIONS: _____

_____

_____

WEATHER: ☐ SUNNY   ☐ PARTLY CLOUDY   ☐ LIGHT OVERCAST   ☐ HEAVY OVERCAST

           ☐ RAIN   ☐ DRIZZLE   ☐ MIST   ☐ FOG   ☐ SLEET   ☐ SNOW

TEMPERATURE: ☐ WARM   ☐ COOL   ☐ COLD   _____ DEGREES

WIND DIRECTION, A.M. _____, P.M. _____ VELOCITY _____ ☐ NO WIND

☐ DECOY SHOOTING   NUMBER OF DECOYS USED: _____ DUCKS _____ GEESE

☐ PASS SHOOTING   CROP RESIDUE (FIELD HUNT) _____

☐ DUCK CALL   ☐ GOOSE CALL   COMMENTS: _____

NOTES: _____

_____

_____

_____

_____

_____

_____

_____

Continued on Next Page

DATE_____

SPECIES BAGGED	NUMBER		COMMENTS
	DRAKES	HENS	
MALLARD			
PINTAIL			
WIDGEON			
GADWALL			
BLUEWING TEAL			
GREENWING TEAL			
SHOVELER			
BLACK DUCK			
WOOD DUCK			
CANVASBACK			
REDHEAD			
BLUEBILL			
RINGBILL			
RUDDY & OTHER			
CANADA GEESE	Greater	Lesser	
WHITE FRONTED GEESE	Adult	Juvenile	
SNOW GEESE			
BLUE GEESE			

☐ BIRD LEG BAND RECOVERED ON SPECIES:_____

NO. ON BAND: _____

☐ REPORTED TO U.S. F&WS ON DATE _____

RESPONSE: BIRD BAND DATE_____ BANDED WHERE?_____

DATE _____

HUNTING PLACE _____

☐ LAKE   ☐ MARSH   ☐ JUMP SHOOTING   ☐ POTHOLES   ☐ SHORELAND   ☐ FIELD HUNT

NEAREST CITY _____

DIRECTION FROM CITY: ☐ N   ☐ S   ☐ E   ☐ W   MILES _____

ARRIVAL TIME _____ DEPARTURE TIME _____

HUNTING COMPANIONS: _____
_____
_____

WEATHER: ☐ SUNNY   ☐ PARTLY CLOUDY   ☐ LIGHT OVERCAST   ☐ HEAVY OVERCAST
           ☐ RAIN   ☐ DRIZZLE   ☐ MIST   ☐ FOG   ☐ SLEET   ☐ SNOW

TEMPERATURE: ☐ WARM   ☐ COOL   ☐ COLD   _____ DEGREES

WIND DIRECTION, A.M._____, P.M._____ VELOCITY_____ ☐ NO WIND

☐ DECOY SHOOTING   NUMBER OF DECOYS USED:_____ DUCKS _____ GEESE

☐ PASS SHOOTING   CROP RESIDUE (FIELD HUNT) _____

☐ DUCK CALL   ☐ GOOSE CALL   COMMENTS: _____

NOTES: _____
_____
_____
_____
_____
_____
_____
_____
_____

Continued on Next Page

DATE_____

SPECIES BAGGED	NUMBER		COMMENTS
	DRAKES	HENS	
MALLARD			
PINTAIL			
WIDGEON			
GADWALL			
BLUEWING TEAL			
GREENWING TEAL			
SHOVELER			
BLACK DUCK			
WOOD DUCK			
CANVASBACK			
REDHEAD			
BLUEBILL			
RINGBILL			
RUDDY & OTHER			
CANADA GEESE	Greater	Lesser	
WHITE FRONTED GEESE	Adult	Juvenile	
SNOW GEESE			
BLUE GEESE			

☐ BIRD LEG BAND RECOVERED ON SPECIES:_____

NO. ON BAND: _____

☐ REPORTED TO U.S. F&WS ON DATE _____

RESPONSE: BIRD BAND DATE_____ BANDED WHERE?_____

DATE _____

HUNTING PLACE _____

☐ LAKE   ☐ MARSH   ☐ JUMP SHOOTING   ☐ POTHOLES   ☐ SHORELAND   ☐ FIELD HUNT

NEAREST CITY _____

DIRECTION FROM CITY: ☐ N   ☐ S   ☐ E   ☐ W   MILES _____

ARRIVAL TIME _____ DEPARTURE TIME _____

HUNTING COMPANIONS: _____
_____
_____

WEATHER: ☐ SUNNY   ☐ PARTLY CLOUDY   ☐ LIGHT OVERCAST   ☐ HEAVY OVERCAST
           ☐ RAIN   ☐ DRIZZLE   ☐ MIST   ☐ FOG   ☐ SLEET   ☐ SNOW

TEMPERATURE: ☐ WARM   ☐ COOL   ☐ COLD   _____DEGREES

WIND DIRECTION, A.M._____, P.M._____   VELOCITY_____   ☐ NO WIND

☐ DECOY SHOOTING   NUMBER OF DECOYS USED:_____DUCKS _____GEESE

☐ PASS SHOOTING   CROP RESIDUE (FIELD HUNT) _____

☐ DUCK CALL   ☐ GOOSE CALL   COMMENTS: _____

NOTES: _____
_____
_____
_____
_____
_____
_____
_____
_____

Continued on Next Page

DATE_____

SPECIES BAGGED	NUMBER		COMMENTS
	DRAKES	HENS	
MALLARD			
PINTAIL			
WIDGEON			
GADWALL			
BLUEWING TEAL			
GREENWING TEAL			
SHOVELER			
BLACK DUCK			
WOOD DUCK			
CANVASBACK			
REDHEAD			
BLUEBILL			
RINGBILL			
RUDDY & OTHER			
CANADA GEESE	Greater	Lesser	
WHITE FRONTED GEESE	Adult	Juvenile	
SNOW GEESE			
BLUE GEESE			

☐ BIRD LEG BAND RECOVERED ON SPECIES:_____

NO. ON BAND: _____

☐ REPORTED TO U.S. F&WS ON DATE _____

RESPONSE: BIRD BAND DATE_____ BANDED WHERE?_____

DATE _____

HUNTING PLACE _____

☐ LAKE　☐ MARSH　☐ JUMP SHOOTING　☐ POTHOLES　☐ SHORELAND　☐ FIELD HUNT

NEAREST CITY _____

DIRECTION FROM CITY:　☐ N　　☐ S　　☐ E　　☐ W　　MILES _____

ARRIVAL TIME _____ DEPARTURE TIME _____

HUNTING COMPANIONS: _____
_____
_____

WEATHER:　☐ SUNNY　☐ PARTLY CLOUDY　☐ LIGHT OVERCAST　☐ HEAVY OVERCAST
　　　　　☐ RAIN　☐ DRIZZLE　☐ MIST　☐ FOG　☐ SLEET　☐ SNOW

TEMPERATURE:　☐ WARM　☐ COOL　☐ COLD　_____ DEGREES

WIND DIRECTION, A.M._____, P.M._____ VELOCITY_____ ☐ NO WIND

☐ DECOY SHOOTING　　NUMBER OF DECOYS USED:_____ DUCKS _____ GEESE

☐ PASS SHOOTING　　CROP RESIDUE (FIELD HUNT) _____

☐ DUCK CALL　　☐ GOOSE CALL　　COMMENTS: _____

NOTES: _____
_____
_____
_____
_____
_____
_____
_____
_____

Continued on Next Page

DATE_____

SPECIES BAGGED	NUMBER		COMMENTS
	DRAKES	HENS	
MALLARD			
PINTAIL			
WIDGEON			
GADWALL			
BLUEWING TEAL			
GREENWING TEAL			
SHOVELER			
BLACK DUCK			
WOOD DUCK			
CANVASBACK			
REDHEAD			
BLUEBILL			
RINGBILL			
RUDDY & OTHER			
CANADA GEESE	Greater	Lesser	
WHITE FRONTED GEESE	Adult	Juvenile	
SNOW GEESE			
BLUE GEESE			

☐ BIRD LEG BAND RECOVERED ON SPECIES:_____

NO. ON BAND: _____

☐ REPORTED TO U.S. F&WS ON DATE _____

RESPONSE: BIRD BAND DATE_____ BANDED WHERE?_____

DATE _____

HUNTING PLACE _____

☐ LAKE ☐ MARSH ☐ JUMP SHOOTING ☐ POTHOLES ☐ SHORELAND ☐ FIELD HUNT

NEAREST CITY _____

DIRECTION FROM CITY: ☐ N ☐ S ☐ E ☐ W MILES _____

ARRIVAL TIME _____ DEPARTURE TIME _____

HUNTING COMPANIONS: _____
_____
_____

WEATHER: ☐ SUNNY ☐ PARTLY CLOUDY ☐ LIGHT OVERCAST ☐ HEAVY OVERCAST
  ☐ RAIN ☐ DRIZZLE ☐ MIST ☐ FOG ☐ SLEET ☐ SNOW

TEMPERATURE: ☐ WARM ☐ COOL ☐ COLD _____ DEGREES

WIND DIRECTION, A.M. _____, P.M. _____ VELOCITY _____ ☐ NO WIND

☐ DECOY SHOOTING NUMBER OF DECOYS USED: _____ DUCKS _____ GEESE

☐ PASS SHOOTING CROP RESIDUE (FIELD HUNT) _____

☐ DUCK CALL ☐ GOOSE CALL COMMENTS: _____

NOTES: _____
_____
_____
_____
_____
_____
_____
_____
_____

Continued on Next Page

DATE_____

SPECIES BAGGED	NUMBER		COMMENTS
	DRAKES	HENS	
MALLARD			
PINTAIL			
WIDGEON			
GADWALL			
BLUEWING TEAL			
GREENWING TEAL			
SHOVELER			
BLACK DUCK			
WOOD DUCK			
CANVASBACK			
REDHEAD			
BLUEBILL			
RINGBILL			
RUDDY & OTHER			
CANADA GEESE	Greater	Lesser	
WHITE FRONTED GEESE	Adult	Juvenile	
SNOW GEESE			
BLUE GEESE			

☐ BIRD LEG BAND RECOVERED ON SPECIES:_____

NO. ON BAND: _____

☐ REPORTED TO U.S. F&WS ON DATE _____

RESPONSE: BIRD BAND DATE_____ BANDED WHERE?_____

DATE _____

HUNTING PLACE _____

☐ LAKE   ☐ MARSH   ☐ JUMP SHOOTING ☐ POTHOLES ☐ SHORELAND   ☐ FIELD HUNT

NEAREST CITY _____

DIRECTION FROM CITY: ☐ N   ☐ S   ☐ E   ☐ W   MILES _____

ARRIVAL TIME _____ DEPARTURE TIME _____

HUNTING COMPANIONS: _____
_____
_____

WEATHER: ☐ SUNNY   ☐ PARTLY CLOUDY   ☐ LIGHT OVERCAST   ☐ HEAVY OVERCAST

           ☐ RAIN   ☐ DRIZZLE   ☐ MIST   ☐ FOG   ☐ SLEET   ☐ SNOW

TEMPERATURE: ☐ WARM   ☐ COOL   ☐ COLD   _____DEGREES

WIND DIRECTION, A.M._____, P.M._____   VELOCITY_____   ☐ NO WIND

☐ DECOY SHOOTING   NUMBER OF DECOYS USED:_____DUCKS _____GEESE

☐ PASS SHOOTING   CROP RESIDUE (FIELD HUNT) _____

☐ DUCK CALL   ☐ GOOSE CALL   COMMENTS: _____

NOTES: _____
_____
_____
_____
_____
_____
_____
_____

Continued on Next Page

DATE_____

SPECIES BAGGED	NUMBER		COMMENTS
	DRAKES	HENS	
MALLARD			
PINTAIL			
WIDGEON			
GADWALL			
BLUEWING TEAL			
GREENWING TEAL			
SHOVELER			
BLACK DUCK			
WOOD DUCK			
CANVASBACK			
REDHEAD			
BLUEBILL			
RINGBILL			
RUDDY & OTHER			
CANADA GEESE	Greater	Lesser	
WHITE FRONTED GEESE	Adult	Juvenile	
SNOW GEESE			
BLUE GEESE			

☐ BIRD LEG BAND RECOVERED ON SPECIES:_____

NO. ON BAND: _____

☐ REPORTED TO U.S. F&WS ON DATE _____

RESPONSE: BIRD BAND DATE_____ BANDED WHERE?_____

DATE _____

HUNTING PLACE _____

☐ LAKE   ☐ MARSH   ☐ JUMP SHOOTING ☐ POTHOLES ☐ SHORELAND   ☐ FIELD HUNT

NEAREST CITY _____

DIRECTION FROM CITY: ☐ N   ☐ S   ☐ E   ☐ W   MILES _____

ARRIVAL TIME _____ DEPARTURE TIME _____

HUNTING COMPANIONS: _____
_____
_____

WEATHER: ☐ SUNNY   ☐ PARTLY CLOUDY   ☐ LIGHT OVERCAST   ☐ HEAVY OVERCAST
           ☐ RAIN   ☐ DRIZZLE   ☐ MIST   ☐ FOG   ☐ SLEET   ☐ SNOW

TEMPERATURE: ☐ WARM   ☐ COOL   ☐ COLD   _____ DEGREES

WIND DIRECTION, A.M. _____, P.M. _____ VELOCITY _____ ☐ NO WIND

☐ DECOY SHOOTING   NUMBER OF DECOYS USED: _____ DUCKS _____ GEESE

☐ PASS SHOOTING   CROP RESIDUE (FIELD HUNT) _____

☐ DUCK CALL   ☐ GOOSE CALL   COMMENTS: _____

NOTES: _____
_____
_____
_____
_____
_____
_____
_____

Continued on Next Page

DATE_____

SPECIES BAGGED	NUMBER		COMMENTS
	DRAKES	HENS	
MALLARD			
PINTAIL			
WIDGEON			
GADWALL			
BLUEWING TEAL			
GREENWING TEAL			
SHOVELER			
BLACK DUCK			
WOOD DUCK			
CANVASBACK			
REDHEAD			
BLUEBILL			
RINGBILL			
RUDDY & OTHER			
CANADA GEESE	Greater	Lesser	
WHITE FRONTED GEESE	Adult	Juvenile	
SNOW GEESE			
BLUE GEESE			

☐ BIRD LEG BAND RECOVERED ON SPECIES:_____

NO. ON BAND: _____

☐ REPORTED TO U.S. F&WS ON DATE _____

RESPONSE: BIRD BAND DATE_____ BANDED WHERE?_____

DATE _____

HUNTING PLACE _____

☐ LAKE   ☐ MARSH   ☐ JUMP SHOOTING   ☐ POTHOLES   ☐ SHORELAND   ☐ FIELD HUNT

NEAREST CITY _____

DIRECTION FROM CITY: ☐ N   ☐ S   ☐ E   ☐ W   MILES _____

ARRIVAL TIME _____ DEPARTURE TIME _____

HUNTING COMPANIONS: _____
_____
_____

WEATHER: ☐ SUNNY   ☐ PARTLY CLOUDY   ☐ LIGHT OVERCAST   ☐ HEAVY OVERCAST
           ☐ RAIN   ☐ DRIZZLE   ☐ MIST   ☐ FOG   ☐ SLEET   ☐ SNOW

TEMPERATURE: ☐ WARM   ☐ COOL   ☐ COLD   _____ DEGREES

WIND DIRECTION, A.M. _____, P.M. _____ VELOCITY _____ ☐ NO WIND

☐ DECOY SHOOTING   NUMBER OF DECOYS USED: _____ DUCKS _____ GEESE

☐ PASS SHOOTING   CROP RESIDUE (FIELD HUNT) _____

☐ DUCK CALL   ☐ GOOSE CALL   COMMENTS: _____

NOTES: _____
_____
_____
_____
_____
_____
_____
_____
_____

Continued on Next Page

DATE _____

SPECIES BAGGED	NUMBER		COMMENTS
	DRAKES	HENS	
MALLARD			
PINTAIL			
WIDGEON			
GADWALL			
BLUEWING TEAL			
GREENWING TEAL			
SHOVELER			
BLACK DUCK			
WOOD DUCK			
CANVASBACK			
REDHEAD			
BLUEBILL			
RINGBILL			
RUDDY & OTHER			
CANADA GEESE	Greater	Lesser	
WHITE FRONTED GEESE	Adult	Juvenile	
SNOW GEESE			
BLUE GEESE			

☐ BIRD LEG BAND RECOVERED ON SPECIES: _____

NO. ON BAND: _____

☐ REPORTED TO U.S. F&WS ON DATE _____

RESPONSE: BIRD BAND DATE _____ BANDED WHERE? _____